MAYA

the

Grand Illusion

By Anil Jain

"This phenomenal world, whatever little one hears or sees of it, the form that is seen, and the form of the seer are all like the horns of a hare."

Ribhu Gita (Chapter 5:2)

Topics

What is Maya?

*Maya desires to find the meaning of her
name, and is set to be surprised by how far
the explanation goes.*

It was evening already, and I left office to reach my home
after my usual five-minute drive. My daughter, Maya came
running to me, with curious look in her eyes. She asked, "Papa,
what is the meaning of my name?"

It was her first day at her school after the end of summer
holidays. She was in the seventh grade. It seems the teachers
had asked all the students to tell something about them. As it
turns out, she was unable to tell much about the meaning of
her name when a student threw the question at her.

I said, "Maya, it seems I will have to write a whole new
book if I were to explain it."

"No way! Do you think I won't have an easy way to tell
people what it means if they ever ask me again?" She asked.

I said, "In easier words, you might say that Maya means an
illusion."

She replied, "I know what an illusion means. Why would you think anyone would require more to know about it?"

I said, "Actually, Maya is not simply an illusion! What if I tell you that You, I and everything that you see around us in this world are nothing but part of the *Maya*, the Grand Illusion!"

She didn't take my reply seriously. She said, "That is the weirdest thing I have heard! How can I or this world be an illusion? I can feel myself along with all the other things around me. I can see my reflection in the mirrors and can feel pain in the body when something hurts. I am very much real."

I kept quiet. I wanted her to say more; think more; question more. We both were quiet for some time. She seemed to get restless. Though she had immediately brushed the idea aside that all reality could simply be an illusion, she was curious to know what explanations I had in my mind to think so. She looked at me and asked, "Even though I don't think what you say makes any sense, I would like to ponder over your idea. It seems so radical! Do you think you can enlighten me about it?"

I said, "Why not! We can start investigating on the nature of the universe right at this very moment. Can you think of a place where we can start?"

She smiled. She said, "I know the game. Let me go and fetch a dictionary. You would want to start it at the beginning, with the definition of the world, illusion, as is generally understood!"

She came back with the dictionary and swiftly browsed through its contents to get to the word which contained the following information.

illusion

noun

1. something that deceives by producing a false or misleading impression of reality
2. *Psychology*. a perception, as of visual stimuli, that represents what is perceived in a way different from the way it is in reality

Maya said, "I think, in simpler words it means to say that an illusion is perceiving reality differently from what it is."

I said, "You said it! Now, would you want to explore more on different words it has used to describe an illusion?"

Maya asked, "You mean – perception, and reality?"

I said, "Yes. Do we know what is meant by perception? Are we also clear about what is reality?"

Maya said, "I think they both are related. Reality is what is, in absolute terms. And a perception is knowing what is, through some means."

I said, "You are doing pretty good! I don't think anyone could easily give such a straight-forward description. So, what are those means through which one perceives the reality?"

Maya replied, "Would it not be our senses?"

I said, "So you do understand that there is a reality around us and that we use our senses to perceive this reality."

Maya said, "Yes. We not only use our five senses to see, hear, touch, taste and smell but also use our memory along with these senses to make sense of the world around us."

I said, "Let's explore what you are saying. You are saying that there is a reality. We are able to know about this reality through our perception of it. We perceive reality through our senses and memory. This is how we know about the reality."

Maya said, "Yes, we know about the reality through our perception of it."

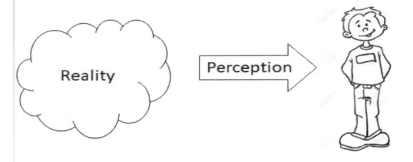

Picture 1: We perceive reality, but do we really know it?

I said, "Let's speak it out loudly in form of a simple example. I see a cup on the table. I touch it and find it hot. It seems filled with a liquid which smells like coffee. My perception of sight, smell and touch created a reality for me, and I perceive a hot cup of coffee on the table. That is my perception and that is my reality too."

Maya agreed, "This is pretty much how things happen."

I asked Maya, "Do you see the inherent confusion about the whole situation already?"

Maya said, "No. I don't know what you are saying."

I said, "Let's go over the situation slowly."

Maya was listening.

Since perceiving is the only way of knowing the reality, we know reality as we perceive it!

I wanted her to start paying attention to the little things that we ordinarily take for granted. We all have taken for granted, the universe and everything it contains. We have become mature and experienced over time, losing much of the sensitivity and compassion in the meantime. We perceive less, think more and decide quickly about everything. We need to learn the art of slowing down, spending some moments with the things in hand, before moving ahead with the next item on our plate.

I said, "The only way we know about the reality is through perception. Is reality simply not all that we perceive?"

Maya said, "Yes, all that we know is all that is true for us."

I asked her, "When everything we perceive is reality, is there a possibility of the reality being different than its perception?"

Maya said, "No. Two things cannot be same and different at the same time. If we smell coffee, we won't believe that it not coffee but is tea instead. In the same way, if we find the cup hot, we won't take the cup to be cool."

I said, "If everything we perceive creates a reality for us, where is the scope for reality to be different than perception? For us, what we perceive is always going to be the reality, Our Reality! But, if this was the only way things had to be, we would never ever be eluded. But we do! We do get deceived, cheated, mesmerized, hypnotized, misunderstood and lied all the times."

Maya said, "I get it now! You are trying to say that everything is a reality in the present moment. It is only later that we might find it an illusion, trick or a deception!"

I said, "That is right! At the time of perception, everything is a reality. One cannot differentiate a reality from an illusion at the time of perceiving.

I was excited as if I had found this for the first time. I said, "Is this not something so mysterious and intriguing?"

Maya seemed to agree. She said, "How true! If that was not the case, there could never be such a thing as an illusion ever. It is only when one's existing belief of reality is broken that one experiences it as an illusion!"

I said, "Is this not exactly how each of us behaves in our daily life? We hold on to our ideas, beliefs and experiences. We find it so hard to accept any suggestions and ideas that contradict our own. We have built our reality based on our perception of it and there is no way we would ever know any difference between the reality as is and the reality as perceived by us. To each of us what we perceive is what there is."

Maya seemed to agree. She had seen many cases of arguments between two people or two groups, each holding

6

their beliefs to be right or superior to other. She was wondering if there was ever a time when we doubted our perceptions and were not sure if things were happening for real.

She asked, "We have agreed that we always know reality through what we are perceiving, but do we also not know at certain times that our perceptions are illusory?"

> "Everything is reality in the present moment. It is only later that we might find it an illusion!"

I said, "Yes, we do know at certain times that what we are perceiving is not the way the reality is. It is because of our memory and learning. That which appears as a lake of water on the distant horizon to the travelers is a well-known illusion that happens in deserts on hot afternoons. People learn about such illusions either by personal experience or after reading or hearing about others' experiences."

Maya said, "I know. When we go to magic shows, we know that there is no way the magician would slice the girl in half. Yet we see the girl cut into two separate parts and both parts seem to be moving. While our perceptions create a reality where the girl is being cut in two pieces, our minds knows that the reality is something different."

Maya continued, "Except for a few occasions where we can see things as an illusion, I find it hard to imagine that this universe and everything it contains is nothing but a big illusion. How can I imagine that nothing could be the way I perceive? If I see a black pencil, a white paper, a brown table or a bird flying in the sky, what would convince me that this all is nothing but *Maya*?"

7

I said, "It is *our* world which is an illusion; the world as we interpret it! Maybe, there is something out there as reality or maybe not. But then, there is definitely something that we make of it; our interpretation, out story, and our world. That creation of ours is the *Maya*, a Grand Illusion!"

Maya said, "If I understand you correctly, you are saying that there are things and movements around, but to know them and treat them specifically, and identifying them as black pencil, white paper, brown table or a flying bird is an illusion."

I said, "You got it."

Maya said, "And why do you think it is something that I or anyone can believe?"

I said, "Let's talk about this. It is not a question of belief. It is all about observing things in great details. If you are sincere in your efforts, you will see all the answers right here, with a thorough investigation on the nature of things and our relationship with them. If you would want to explore about this complex issue, we can start from some very basic illusions and make our way toward more complex ones."

Maya said, "I would love to know more."

I said, "Let's wrap up our today's discussion with what we learnt today. Since every perception is always a reality to the perceiver at that moment, a few of which could be found to be illusory later, we can identify this fact from our investigation."

Then I wrote on the whiteboard hanging on the wall.

All Illusion was once a Reality.

2

Illusions that we have created

The world in which we live is a creation of
our imagination.

There are two kinds of ignorance when facing the reality of our universe. The first kind of ignorance is to be always assured that the reality is exactly as being perceived. A few days back I had spent some time with Maya and talked over a few scenarios where we know that reality might be different than what our senses tell us. When we are in a desert on a hot and sunny afternoon, a sight of possible water in the horizon is most probably an illusion. When we wake up after spending a few hours of what we perceive as a reality, we are surprised to find that it was just a dream. All the perceptions during dream state look real but are not.

We exist in a dynamic universe where everything is changing in a chaotic way. If we were to try to understand and make sense of anything that goes around in this world, we would not have a single clue about the smallest thing out there. This is where the origin of the second kind of ignorance can be seen. We are not comfortable with the universe changing shapes and refreshing itself continuously. In our quest to understand this dynamic reality with certainty, we came up with some illusory ideas about it. Those ideas give us a sense of permanency, certainty and uniformity. We have accustomed ourselves of using those ideas to observe our world at all times like a child wearing a toy goggle made of colored glasses. Those ideas show us a heavily twisted and partial view of the universe in the same way as the colored goggles made of a cheap plastic show to a child. With a red film on the goggles, the child views everything as red, and with a wavy surface of the plastic film, everything appears distorted to the child. Over time, as we continue to observe the reality in a specific way, we get accustomed to this imagined reality as reality itself and forget that it was a creation of our mind.

I sat down with Maya today again and continued with the discussion we had started some time back on the nature of illusions in this world. I told her that we should not be surprised about the illusory nature of the universe, especially when more than half of all our illusions are our own creation.

She was surprised. She asked me if I could tell her more.

I said, "We have created three major illusions."
1. Even though we encounter a continuous unbroken reality, we imagine divisions in it.
2. We exist in an absolute reality, but cannot go beyond perceiving it in relative terms.
3. We created imaginary shapes and try to fit all perceived reality to conform to them.

She asked me to confirm, "Are you saying that we have ourselves created an illusion of divisions, shapes and relative understanding of what is, otherwise, a continuous and absolute reality?

10

I said, "Yes, this is what I am saying. We have not only imagined these illusions, but have also been successfully transferring this knowledge through future generations by educating and training them.

Maya asked, "You mean to say that half of our illusions are the product of our education? Wouldn't that make an illiterate person in the remote village of a third world country less illusory?"

I said, "Oh, that is certainly so! Anyone who hasn't been exposed to formal education and much of our society would be more in touch with reality because of his or her innate ability to respond to the universe using intuition and unconditioned mind."

We have ourselves created an illusion of divisions, shapes and relative understanding of what is otherwise, a continuous and absolute reality.

Maya said, "Then I would certainly like to know what sort of illusions we have accustomed ourselves by undergoing formal education."

I said, "Would you even doubt if the reality is ever unbroken anywhere? Whether you look at our body, or a plant or even the planet itself, you wouldn't find any divisions anywhere. If you observe our planet keenly, you would find that all of its surface is continuous. Yet, we have created countless imaginary divisions and called them as nations, states, cities and towns. When you travel in an airplane, you may find a screen with flight map in front of you showing the country or the city you are flying over. But when you look down from the window, do you see any such separation in the continuous land?"

Maya said, "Obviously not. All the boundaries marking the separation on a piece of land on earth is a human imagination."

I said, "Do you think once imagined, such separation of the land between various countries, towns or cities are even permanent?"

Maya said, "All these ideas of separate land are not even permanent. They change their shapes and ownership on daily basis."

I asked Maya, "With just one example of our illusory division of land into separate lands, can we see if we are more intelligent than birds, animals, insects or even not so literate humans living in the far corners of the world?"

Maya said, "Certainly not! A bird wouldn't have an issue crossing over an imaginary division of the land, whereas a person might be confined to prison for many years for doing the same. That strange behavior is definitely only a human one."

She then asked, "I can understand that there is literally no separation on the land, but what about the continents or islands that are truly separated. Do you think identifying them as separate piece of land is an illusion too?"

I asked, "You mean separated by water?"

She said, "Yes. Wouldn't you say Australia and Africa are two separate pieces of lands."

I asked, "They sure look separate but are they really separate? Don't they both share one continuous land, part of which is submerged under the ocean? If you were to stand in neck deep water with your hands out, would you treat the visible parts of your two hands as separated and ignore the fact that they are joined to one single body under the water?"

I added, "It may be understandable that the two islands may give an illusion of separation. But it makes absolutely no sense to view one continuous body of ocean as separate oceans."

Maya said, "I get it. All divisions in the lands and oceans are man-made illusions. It does not matter if the boundary of the land is imaginary or visibly separate due to presence of water, it is simply one continuous surface of our planet."

I said, "The way we divided piece of land and oceans, we also came up with an idea of dividing the time. Time is an illusion created by the very act of dividing the continuity and giving it a fixed dimension. We came up with the ideas of days, hours, minutes and seconds to create an imagination of a predictable and uniform universe, *Our* World."

Maya said, "I can see now how much of our real life is already influenced by illusions which are our own creation. We live in illusory boundaries of nations, thereby creating illusory nature of friends and enemies. We keep track of activities in our lives in terms of durations such as days, months, years which have no real existence in the nature. I say it because if my age was dependent only on how many revolutions my planet made around the sun, then I would have a different age on different planets of our solar system! It seems all these efforts that we made are only good enough for our comfortable survival on this particular planet."

I said, "That was a good observation! All our knowledge and learning is specific to the planet we live on. It has nothing to do with the absolute reality."

Maya said, "This was the first kind of illusion which we ourselves created by assuming discontinuity in a continuous reality. You talked about the other one where mentioned something about absolute and relative knowledge. I would like to know about that too."

I asked, "Yes. We can talk about that too. You know that we perceive reality in our attempt to know it; right?"

Maya said, "Yes, that is right."

I asked, "What do you mean by 'knowing'?"

Maya said, "To know means to understand."

I said, "Are we clear about what we mean by understanding?"

Maya said, "Let me think what we mean by understanding. If I look at something or hear or touch, I want to know what it is. I may also want to know how it is in comparison to other things."

I said, "Can we say that in trying to understand something that we perceive, all we are doing is measuring and comparing?"

Maya said, "I am not sure if this is what we are doing all the time."

I said, "Let's take an example. What happens when you look somewhere and you notice something? You either recognize it or do you don't. Whether you recognize it or not, you have compared that which you have noticed to what you have already known through similar observation in the past and have a memory of its association with a name, quality and experience about it. So, when you try to know what you see, you measure and compare it with something known. If you are able to compare, you say you know about it. On the contrary, if you are unable to measure or compare, you say that you don't' know about it. But in any case, your ability to know or not know an observation always includes measurement and comparison."

Maya said, "I think I get it."

I said, "When you compare something with other, are you observing in absolute terms or in relative terms?"

Maya said, "If I compare two things, then all I am noticing is the difference between the two. I am not looking at the absolute qualities in any one."

I said, "That is right. If I compare the intelligence of two people and say that one is smarter than other, I don't know in absolute terms how intelligent any one of them is."

Maya said, "So you are saying that there is no time we can ever know anything absolute about anything."

I said, "When knowing itself means viewing relatively, then where is the question of knowing absolutely?

Maya said, "I can understand it that the description of knowing involves viewing things in comparison. But that doesn't convince me that there doesn't exist any other kind of knowledge that could be absolute. "

I said, "What is there to know about anything? Is the idea of knowing simply not an illusion? Let me take an example. You want to know what the

"An absolute knowledge is an illusion. It makes no sense for the skin to measure its own temperature."

temperature of the room is. What is a temperature? Can you ever know (absolutely) the temperature of anything? Is a temperature not an expression of hotness or coolness of a surface? How do you determine this hotness or coolness? Is it not the relative feeling compared to the temperature of your own skin? The idea of absolute temperature is just an illusion. From the point of view of your body, the temperature of the skin is the absolute temperature. All you can notice is the relative feeling in comparison to this absolute temperature. You can never know the absolute value. An absolute knowledge is an illusion. It makes no sense for the skin to measure its own temperature. An observer capable of observing itself is an illusory idea."

I continued, "Whether it is the temperature, weight, volume, color or any other criteria on basis of which we want to perceive the reality, all of them involve comparing the observed quality with some predefined standard. That predefined standard value is nothing but an imaginary value which everyone agrees to. For example, the standard value of one kilogram is assumed to be the weight of a prototype made with platinum-iridium alloy kept at a museum in Paris. When we say something weighs exactly one kilogram, we mean to say that it's as heavy as that prototype."

Maya said, "I seem to have learned everything you said in my school, yet we were never able to look at the world in this way. It is so true! We can only observe a reality, never make sense out of it. Because making sense or acquiring knowledge involves at least two things for making a comparison, one of which must be already known. It is like a paradox, where a prior knowledge must already exist in order to know something new."

I said, "We have already seen that we created illusory ideas about distinction and separation in our continuous world and created a never-ending conflict between humans based on geographic location, race, color and language. We have also created an idea of knowledge and learning everything we perceive by comparing and evaluating them with some illusory values. We are unaware that what we understand is true only from our own unique perspective because all learning involves comparison of the new with our own previous learning."

Having made my point about our limited idea of knowing and understanding the reality of our universe, I proceeded to tell Maya about the third man-made illusion. I said, "The third illusion that I mentioned, is the idea of geometric shapes which we use for observing the universe as well as creating an illusory world for us."

Maya said, "Creating an illusory world? I didn't understand."

I said, "All geometry is an illusion. We use geometry to observe the reality and understand it. You must have studied this in your schools. Do you know what a Point is?"

Maya said, "A point is some location with no size; it has no width, length or depth."

I said, "A location with no size! Do we need to say more?"

Maya smiled. She said, "Now I understand why you said all geometry is an illusion. We know that a point is an illusion. It is simply an idea with no actual existence which could be seen, felt or understood. Then we created a concept of a line which is made of countless dots or points which themselves have no existence. We also created the idea of all other shapes such as triangle, quadrilateral, pentagon and circle, all of which are made of either lines or curves made of countless points."

I said, "We create illusory ideas that suit us. Those ideas suit us because they provide us a child's play goggle with colored glasses to see the world in the color we desire. When we look at the irregular shape or earth, never ending continuous stretch of oceans, land or time, we find ourselves in a desperate situation of helplessness. We need to have simple geometric shapes around us to please us, ones which are illusory. So, we create straight roads, straight poles, walls, buildings, papers, books. When we see a peculiar formation in the nature, we try to fit it with some mathematical formulas We also need to know the sequence of events, so we break the time into discrete parts. In our pursuit to create our own version of the universe, we try to act God. It turns out that we are not very good at that."

Maya said, "I understand now, what you meant when you said that we create illusory world. In our attempt to make sense out of irregular, dynamic and highly unpredictable nature of the reality, we have imagined and constructed our own version of a regular, uniform, repeating and predictable reality."

I smiled. Suddenly Maya remembered something. I saw her going towards the whiteboard and writing this.

An observer capable of observing itself is an illusory idea.

3

Illusions that we know

We live in the world surrounded by
numerous illusions that we are already aware
of.

I wanted to pick my discussion with Maya from where we left last time on the topic of illusions and the nature of universe around us. We both had agreed that it was simply not possible for one to be aware of a possible illusion while perceiving the world around us unless we had a memory of some past knowledge or experience of similar nature. The discussion started when I told her that her name referred to the Grand Illusion of the Universe around us, which she did not find worth believing. I thought we might as well talk about things that she could believe, such as the illusions that are already known to us.

I asked Maya, "Do you know how many ways we would encounter illusions in our daily life?"

Maya said, "I can remember quite some of them, thought I am not sure if I could easily differentiate one from other on some specific ground."

I said, "That's ok. We will start talking about them. We might be able to notice their peculiarity, once we have brought up a few of them."

Maya said, "As I said last time, the Mirage is one of those illusions where one can see water on a hot afternoon on a distance in desert. We also talked about magic shows where the magician cuts a girl in half, or makes it vanish from under a big sheet of cloth."

She continued, "I hope we could call a rainbow an illusion too, because there is really no specific thing as a colored arch as it usually shows up when there is a moisture in the air and the sun is at some specific area in the sky."

I said, "Yes, I too hope that we can call a rainbow, an illusion. We know that in reality there is only sunlight and water vapor in the sky. But in our perception, there are different colors in form of an arch, which has no real existence."

As I said this, I could see how we could classify the different illusions we already know about. I said to Maya, "Is a rainbow not an illusion, because we perceive a form when there is none (in reality)?"

Maya said, "That would be right."

"Let's then make if our first kind of an Illusion."

Illusion 1 - Perceiving a form when there is none.

I asked Maya if she can think of all the kinds of illusions where one tends to perceive a form which is not there.

She said, "I think I remember something. When we see some dots arranged in a particular order, we identify the overall pattern as a square rather than a group of dots. When some of the dots in the same arrangement are moved a little, we see a circle."

Picture 2: This arrangement of dots is seen as shapes representing a square and a circle.

It was one fine example of illusion of forms. We all know that we perceive visual information through our eyes. When the eyes encounter too much things to deal with at any moment, they cannot process everything that appears in the field of vision as it is. Instead, in trying to comprehend what is seen, it merges the prominent noticeable things in form of one single abstraction. As a result, what is seen by the eyes at any given moment is not the reality but an idea of the reality from the observer's point of view.

Our senses of vision are limited both in space and time. While their limitation in space gives rise to the illusion of forms, their limitation of handling large amount of data in a given time gives rise to the illusion of movement. I asked Maya, "Do you know what you see in a video, television or a movie is also an illusion?"

Maya said, "Yes, we all know this yet we don't really care much because we are mostly busy with the story part of what we observe. Is it not true that a real-time experience of movements in any video or a movie is actually made up of a larger number of still images made to appear one after another very quickly in front of our eyes?"

I agreed. Suddenly I remembered something. I asked, "Do you remember flip books?"

Maya said, "Oh yeah! Even I have made some in the past. You flip through the pages fast and can see the animation effect from the individual pictures."

Picture 3: A Flip Book shows the images in motion

I asked Maya, "What kind of illusion is it when a lot of still images seen in a very short time appear to be moving?"

She said, "That would be an illusion of movement."

I thought it was time to register a second kind of illusion.

Illusion 2 - Perceiving a movement when there is none.

The inadequacy of handling a lot of data in a very short time is limited not only to the eyes, but also to all other sense organs. When we listen to the sound of a single violin through our ears, we hear a crisp sound of a single violin. Later when twenty more violinists start playing at the same time, our ears don't hear the sound of twenty separate violins playing individually. Instead what they hear is a composite sound made by merging of all individual sounds, which is felt very different than a single violin's sound. Like the eyes, the ears too cannot process many separate pieces of information available to them. In combining all that is heard from several sources, the ears seem to form a new 'shape' of the sound.

I told Maya, "Can you think of any other example of illusion of movement besides movies and television?"

She said, "Yes, I can think of human-wave in the stadiums."

It was a good example. Human wave is the effect observed in crowded stadiums when a section of stands up with raised arms and then sits down as the next section of people repeats the action. There appears to be a huge ripple moving amidst the ocean made of people. When seen from a distance, the eyes are unable to capture and grasp each individual human movement separately. Instead they merge all those fast-moving individual pieces and grasps a much bigger but slower movement, the human wave. An illusion of movement when there is none!

Maya said, "Is the Domino's effect also an illusion of movement?"

I said, "Yes, quite literally so. In case of the dominos too, the time delay in falling of each set of subsequent dominos seems like a part of a single travelling ripple among the cascade of falling domino pieces. Any example of ripple movement would be the case of an illusion of movement"

Maya said, "I don't think that is true in all cases. What about the actual ripples in water? I don't think that is an illusion!"

I said, "Ripples in the water are also an illusion."

Maya didn't believe. How could a ripple in water be an illusion? She said, "When we drop a pebble in water, we can clearly see that many ripples start from where the pebble is dropped travelling outward creating big circles on the surface of water. If this were to be an illusion, then the moving ripple could not have a real existence. If they had an illusory form, how can we explain the force that the moving ripples present? Don't we see huge damage that the moving waves cause in an ocean? How could a wave be an illusion? We have ourselves seen the amount of damage that the tsunami waves cause on the sea shores."

I said, "A stadium wave or a wave in the falling dominos is a crude illustration of how a wave gets created in the ocean. The only difference is that in case of ocean, there are billions and billions of water particles in each wave compared to a few hundred humans in a stadium wave. Therefore, it is easier to accept a human wave to be an illusion, but not the waves in the ocean. If you can see, the falling dominos are able to create a moving force which can make an impact at the point of contact of the last piece in the falling chain. The impact is real, even though the wave is an illusion."

26

Maya seemed to understand but couldn't grasp it. It was easy to see and grasp an illusion in one case, but not in the other.

I let her settle into her newly acquired knowledge for some time. It was just the beginning. Our exploration into the nature of things and our perception of them were going to open many more surprises for her. She was soon going to begin seeing that the world that we perceive was nowhere close to reality.

It had been a few minutes before any of us spoke. I looked at her and saw that she was ready to take our conversation ahead.

I said, "We have understood that our sensory perceptions are limited in time and space and cannot handle too many changes or too fast changes. Our bodies have been designed to create a meaningful interpretation of all that happens within such limitations of our sense organs. This interpretation allows us to get a vague idea about the reality, not the actual reality."

I thought of doing a little experiment. I showed her a picture.

I said, "Look at this picture. What do you think it is?"

Picture 4: A shape may look different when seen in a mirror. But it is seen as the same thing by the mind

She looked and said, "It is the letter 'P'."

27

I asked her, "They both are 'P'; Right?"

She nodded. She was aware that the other symbol was the reflection of the letter 'P' in the mirror.

I showed her another picture in which I used the same mirror image of letter 'P' to create a word.

I asked her, "What is the first letter in this word?"

She said, "It is a 'Q'."

quit

Picture 5: The first letter is a P written as its mirror image, but is still seen as a Q, because that makes sense.

I asked, "Why did you say it is a 'Q'? I wrote it literally using the letter P on my keyboard by creating its mirror image."

She said, "It does not matter how you wrote it. It is a Q."

I asked, "Would you agree that all that you perceive is all of your reality here, even though you know it is different than the reality?"

She said, "Yes, that's true. It may be a 'P' in reality, but it appears as a 'Q' here because that only makes sense here."

I asked, "Can we call is yet another kind of illusion?"

She said, "I think so. Would that be an illusion of context and meaning?"

I said, "Yes. Imagine you have this letter imprinted on a transparent piece of a square sheet and lying on the floor as if it fell from a child's toy set. Would you want to imagine if it is a 'P', 'q', 'b' or a 'd'? Or would you just look at it as it is and not bother about its meaning?"

She said, "Lying on its own, and having no context I would not try to guess what it is. It could be anything. I might not even think if it has a meaning, because it could possibly be some symbol with a totally different interpretation than what I might assume."

I said, "So we already know that we tend to look at things different than the reality itself based on their context and the meaning." We noted our third kind of illusion.

Illusion 3 – Perceiving a meaning when there is none.

I said, "We all have an obsession to find meaning and purpose of things. When we look around at things which are in agreement to our past experiences or our beliefs, we are relieved. On the other hand, when things don't make sense, we are worried, and stressed. Things in the universe are always moving, happening and changing with the forces unknown to us. Nevertheless, we never stop coming up with reasons using what is known as 'science, which tries to bind everything in the realm of purpose and meaning. What seems to make sense to an Englishman might not make sense to an Asian if he knows no other language than his own. A written text which might make one person angry might have no effect on the other.

Things don't have a meaning; it is up to the person observing them to make sense."

We are aware of this quality of ours. We are not only able to create forms and shapes when there are none, but we are also able to associate names with those forms and shapes, and later recreate an idea about them just by recalling their names. When I talk about a square to somebody, the image of a square shape comes into the other person's mind. I don't have to draw a shape or bring a picture of a square every time I talk about it.

Our abilities don't just stop at recognizing the forms and shape and associating them with their names. When no such shape exists as in case of random dots, we are able to view them as shapes due to the limitation of our eyes in keeping all the fine details separate. As soon as a shape is recognized, we are able to give a meaning to those shapes based on our past experience and memory. We not only see the dots as some shapes, but we are also able to recognize the shapes carrying some meaning such as words of a language or digits of some numbers.

ABCDEFGHIJKLMNO
PQRSTUVWXYZÀÁÄÊÍ
abcdefghijklmnop

Picture 6: All electronic displays, screens and computer prints are nothing but random dots, seen carrying message because of an illusion of shape and meaning created due to limitation of our perception.

30

This illusion comes in handy with all the electronic displays such as television, computer monitors, printers and advertisement displays. They contain nothing but a random sequencing of dots changing at high pace, giving us an illusion of moving pictures, letters and words.

I started thinking. So far, we talked about perceiving a form or a movement when there was none. We also thought of some illusions of meaning and interpretation when there would not be any. Before we talked about any of them, we thought of mirage, the illusion of water in the desert. I don't think it might be classified under any of the three kinds we discussed. It was a case of perceiving one thing for another. It was a case of mistaken identity, where a form was perceived but given a different meaning than the reality. In case of a mirage, the refraction of light in the desert gives an impression of water. I asked Maya if she knew of any example beside a mirage where people got confused by a thing for another.

She replied, "I have heard that sometimes at night, you might fear a rope, as if it is a snake."

"How true!" I thought. It seemed like we had encountered yet another kind of illusion.

Illusion 4 – Creating a reality by perceiving a thing for another.

I told Maya, "We started talking about the illusions that we all are aware of and agree to their existence. As we came across the examples, we tried to find the underlying reasons which makes them illusions. Those underlying reasons were our habits of perceiving forms, movements or meanings in the places where there might be none really."

31

After summarizing what we had found out so far, I asked her, "Do you recall any other examples of illusions besides the ones that we talked?"

Maya said, "What of the Tooth Fairy, the Santa, or the God?"

I said, "They seem to be even bigger illusions, as there is absolutely no perception involved in them. All the ones we talked about till now were because of imperfect perception of the reality. Whereas these ones are just ideas originating from the human mind and have been taken as a reality. This definitely calls for, yet another way people can experience an illusion."

Illusion 5 – Creating a reality from an idea, without perceiving.

Maya said, "Don't you think calling God an illusion can make people angry?

I said, "So does calling a Tooth Fairy or the Santa unreal, which can make the kids go crazy!"

Maya understood. There has never ever been a perception which created a reality of a Santa or the Tooth Fairy, but that alone is not sufficient reason for the kids not to believe in them. They have been told stories about them so many times, that those characters are not illusions any more, they are real. She got up and started writing on the whiteboard.

Things don't have a meaning. We make it up.

Whodunnit?

When the source of movements is explored,
Maya wonders if there ever was an action,
the root of all actions, which was not
dependent on some prior cause.

We were sitting in the garden under a tree. While I was busy reading a book, I felt something strike on my head. Bewildered by the sudden pain, I looked around to see what hit me. There was a dried-out lemon, that had fallen from above. It might purely be a matter of chance that it fell, or it could possibly be due to some bird activity on the tree. There was really no reason to be annoyed, especially as there was no one to put a blame on.

As I tried to get my attention back to what I was doing, I could not help but to notice something weird. No, it was not the feeling of the pain that was still there in my head. The weirdness of the situation was in the feeling of helplessness. Something had happened just now and I was hurt, but surprisingly there was no one to be blamed, or punished. Maya looked at me and said, "You seem to be thinking about something."

I said, "This lemon fell on my head, and I am not sure if I understand anything that seems to be happening in this universe!"

Maya said, "I don't get it! What is so confusing about the lemon falling on your head?"

I said, "If something has happened, then someone must have done it, right?"

Maya said, "That is right. Nothing can happen on its own."

I said, "I am confused about how and on whom to put the ownership of this action, or any action for that matter?"

Maya said, "I still don't understand what your confusion is about? You got hurt by a lemon falling from the tree. It is usual to see things like this happen at times."

I said, "What I find weird here is that there is no one to put blame upon. Now I am confused if I am ever sure about any action going on around us and not just this one in particular."

Maya said, "I still don't understand your confusion."

I said, "Do you think it is the fault of the lemon? It was the one to directly hit my head and cause me the pain."

Maya said, "The immediate cause for the pain is surely the lemon. But how can it bear the responsibility for the action?"

I said, "Why not?"

Maya said, "A lemon has no consciousness. It cannot know."

I said, "You mean it lacks awareness?"

Maya said, "That is right. A lemon is not aware that something is happening."

I said, "Let's assume that the lemon had an awareness that it fell and hurt me on my head. Does that make it responsible for the hurt?"

Maya said, "Not if it didn't intentionally jump on your head to hurt you. It's fall has to be dependent upon something else."

I asked, "You mean to say that it lacked intention to hurt me?"

Maya said, "Right. It lacked the intention."

I said, "You made some very good observations. You are saying that something or someone cannot be the owner of a task, the real actor responsible for an activity if it doesn't have the necessary intention as well as awareness."

Maya asked, "And if there is no intention or awareness, then it must be dependent on something else which might have caused it to act in certain way. Do you think intention and awareness are both needed for something or someone to be the actor of a task? Is intention alone without an awareness not sufficient enough to ensure that it does not need to depend on other causes to act?"

I said, "That is a good question. Let us try to think over it. Let us say that the lemon had an intent of jumping over me. Could it be possible that it was not aware of what it was doing? Sure, if it was brain-washed by some lemon-specific religion assuming that all humans are worthless, it might have an

35

intention but no awareness. The question is whether such a lemon can be called the real actor behind the action?"

Maya said, "If there is such a scenario then lemon has no awareness. It has no idea why it wanted to hurt you except that it has been taught to hate you and hurt you. Such an intention, which is conditioned by some other knowledge, cannot be the true intention. In fact, in such a scenario it is behaving just like a dumb machine, being operated by the conditioning it has been trained or commanded with."

I said, "There you go! So, if the intent is corrupted by some sort of conditioning, it should be seen as 'dependent' on the conditioning. Therefore, such a conditioned intent cannot be called as the real actor behind any action. Would you say the lemon was the real culprit behind the action if it was absolutely free of any conditioning and just wanted to land on my head?"

Maya said, "In that case, the lemon truly has an intent to fall on your head, but not of hurting you. It has no such awareness."

I said, "You seem to be right. Only when the lemon knew it well that it wanted to hurt me, would I know that the lemon was the real actor behind the action. If the lemon just wanted to land on my head, it cannot be called as the real cause for hurting me. In such a case, the intent to hurt was missing.

Maya said, "So, it is settled! Both unconditioned intent, and the awareness of the action are required for something or someone to be called an owner of an action."

I said, "That's right."

Maya asked, "Now that I get it, I am still wondering what was the sense of weirdness about the lemon falling from the tree? You already found out that there was nobody that hurt you."

I said, "Why do you say there was nobody? There must be someone responsible for hurting me. Would you not put the blame on the tree, or on a bird? There should be someone on whom the lemon's fall depended on."

Maya said, "Did we not discuss just now? A tree or a bird lacks both the intention as well as the awareness. How can one be responsible for an action which one has no awareness or intention?"

I said, "That is right! I know that it was neither the tree nor any bird that intended to hit me with a lemon. That is what worries me. When I saw that there was nobody to be called responsible for the action that happened here, I could not put the blame on anyone or anything. Now I am no longer sure if I ever know any single action which can be attributed to someone or something with an intent or awareness. The whole universe is operating, yet there is no one actually doing anything."

Maya said, "I don't understand how you can suddenly compare this example with the whole universe! You can't compare lemon or a bird to humans. We have the intelligence as well as awareness. Do we not satisfy both the conditions for being the actors behind all of our actions?"

I said, "Let us try to explore this situation thoroughly. Once we have done that, we might be able to apply our learning to everything else around us."

Maya liked the idea. She was still not sure how I could suddenly start doubting the intelligence of whole human civilization just by noticing an accidental fall of a non-living object. She knew that I go to work every day and get paid for the work I do. If I wasn't responsible for the work and there were such doubts in the minds of the company management, why would I get paid if I was not the real doer of my tasks? She wasn't sure where the confusion was about finding out the real actor behind any action.

I asked, "What is the situation here?"

Maya said, "A lemon fell on your head and you feel pain."

I said, "I was reading a book and I noticed pain in the head. I immediately found out that a lemon had hit me. The action that happened was surely 'hitting on the head'. So, I am trying to figure out who the actor was? Was it the lemon?"

Maya said, "Even though the lemon hit you and hurt you directly, the lemon is not the real actor behind your pain. We have seen that a real ownership of an action lies with the one with an unconditional intent and awareness."

I asked, "What can we say about the action that happened here? Something that happened without awareness and intent."

An unconditioned intent with awareness is the real actor behind all actions.

Maya said, "We can only say that the lemon had no intent. It fell due to some other reason."

I asked, "If the lemon didn't fall intentionally, can we say that lemon's fall was dependent on something else?

Maya said, "Oh, yes! It had no intent of its own. It was definitely depending on something else for that 'push' which made it fall."

I said, "So, what we are saying is that anything that is dependent on something else cannot have a real intent to carry out an action independently. All such actions can be rightly said to be responses, which ought to be triggered by some prior action."

Maya said, "Yes. That seems right."

I said, "And as long as any action was not carried out with an independent intention and awareness, the action cannot be truly attributed to such an actor."

Maya said, "That seems right too! Because, like you said, all such actions would be some form of responses of some prior action."

I asked, "Do you know why we want to find out whether an action is dependent or independent?"

Maya asked, "Is it to find the real cause of the action?"

I said, "Yes. First, we would want to know the real driver behind the action if we need to have control over a situation. Second, we would also want to know if an action is a dependent one, so that we don't waste our time on analyzing such actions because they are really the responses of some other action."

Maya said, "Won't it be easy to understand if we had some examples?"

I said, "Let's imagine, a liquid is boiling and spilling out of the pot. Would you put a lid over it to stop spilling?"

Maya said, "Putting the lid or pouring some more liquid might solve the issue temporarily, but a correct way would be to know that the source of the action is the heat from the stove. In other words, the spilling liquid is the response and the heat is the actor. If we switch off the stove or move the vessel away from the heat, we would have tackled the issue rightfully because we have worked with the real actor behind the ultimate action."

I said, "So, we do know that acting directly on those actions which are dependent on some other action does not serve us rightfully. Such actions are simply the response borne out of some other prior action. The source of spilling was the heat, and not the liquid itself. Acting on the liquid to cover it up or adding more liquid would not be an appropriate solution to the problem."

Maya said, "I know. It is same as someone trying to open up the windows or using fans to push the smoke out of the room, but not paying attention to the real cause of the smoke, which is the fire burning in the corner of the room. As long as you focus on the smoke, the problem will continue no matter how many tricks you use, because smoke is a response of the fire. Working on eliminating the fire will ensure that the problem of the smoke slowly and steadily comes to its natural end."

Maya paused for a moment and then said, "I remember a quotation, where it was mentioned that when the cart doesn't move, you don't whip the cart."

I smiled. I said, "That is right. The movement of cart is dependent on the horse. The horse is the actor which moves the cart. If the horse is made to move, the cart will move. Whipping the cart will not only be ineffective, it will be stupid."

I said, "Knowing any action as dependent on other causes is to break the illusion of the perceived actor. A dependent action is simply a response. Taking a response as an actor is our illusion. We might seem to get reasonable results by working on such illusory actors which are nothing but responses of other actions. However, such results are achieved only at the cost of wasting more energy and effort than required if we knew the real actor behind all actions."

> **"Knowing any action as dependent on other causes is to break the illusion of the perceived actor."**

Picture 7: Action 2 cannot be the real driver, because it is dependent on Action 1. Action 1 is the real driver, as long as it is independent of any other action.

Maya asked, "Does it mean that an intent is not dependent on anything?"

I corrected her, "An unconditioned intent."

Maya said, "Oh, yes. A conditioned intent would depend on the conditioning. In other word, a conditioned intent is like

41

a response of some other causes. Only an unconditioned intent can be said to be a truly independent entity."

I said, "It has become so simple now. Any activity which is independent, is the root cause and the owner of subsequent action; the Creator behind the Creation; the Intent."

Maya said, "Are you worried, because you think that there is no activity that is totally independent? Are you worried that we have an illusion about the action and the actor in this world? Do you mean to say that existence of a driver with an independent intent is yet another myth in the world; nothing but a Grand Illusion!"

I said, "THAT is my worry! If you look closely, you won't find a single example of unconditioned intent with awareness. Just check around and let me know if you find me wrong."

Maya said, "In our example of the cart, we said that the cart wouldn't move if whipped, because it is dependent on the horse. Do we not know that the horse lacks the intent, and the real driver of the cart and the horse is the person whipping the horse? Why would you not be satisfied to have found the source of this action and the intent with the human who is riding the cart? Does he not have the intention as well as awareness to make the cart move?"

I said, "It is true that he has the intention and the awareness and therefore, satisfies our criteria of being the one to drive the horse-cart. In its simplest form, if the world was made of only these three entities, we would already have come to a right conclusion. But the universe is vast, and there are countless objects which are always interacting with each other. On such a grand stage, the intention of the cart-man to move the cart cannot be called an unconditioned intention. His intention to move the cart must be dependent upon the reasons for which he needs to move the cart. The source of this action cannot simply end with the cart man. It goes to the source of his desires, his needs, his urgencies, and his helplessness. All desires are dependent on some end goal to be accomplished. A person desiring to pursue an act cannot be said to be having an unconditioned intent.

Maya said, "Oh! I can see that he might have some reason for making the cart move, the reason on which his intention depends. Is it not possible that he would have wanted to take the cart somewhere for no specific purpose in mind? It could be a purposeless wandering. Many times, we do things for no real reason."

I said, "I would doubt if someone would take a horse-cart for a purposeless wandering. I would prefer to take just the horse instead. Even if one is riding the horse purposelessly, one would not need to whip the horse. With no purpose in mind, the horse and the rider would be in a harmony, going nowhere in particular and with no intent. You whip the horse if you want it to move. That is surely a purpose. In a purposeless wandering, there would be nobody riding or going somewhere. There would be no one to make the intent, and no one to see the fulfilment of the intent."

Maya said, "I see what you were worried about. You are saying that there cannot be an action free of conditioning. To all the action going around, it is hard to point to a single intent which truly drives it, without being dependent on other causes."

She then asked, "What about an action which is partially dependent on outside causes? Is it equally wrong to treat a partially dependent action as the primary cause of actions?"

I said, "It should not matter if an action is totally dependent or partially dependent on other causes. As long as there is a dependence, however insignificant, the intent is not free of conditioning and cannot be called an independent cause for the actions. Let's imagine a heart surgeon. For him to be able to operate on the patient, he needs a team of people who can take care of keeping the patient under anesthesia, monitoring the blood pressure and checking the functioning of all other vital body organs while the surgeon works on the heart. Even though it is a team effort, it is always the heart surgeon who is credited for the successful heart operation while every other form of dependency is ignored and forgotten. Can you believe if the surgeon would be able to carry out the operation if everything was ready except for one single thing, which could be the anesthesiologist, or the blood pressure monitoring system?"

Maya said, "There definitely won't be any operation if there was no anesthesiologist. I see it now. If something is dependent on ten different things, then removing nine of the dependencies doesn't do any good. For something to be independent, every little piece of dependency needs to go away."

Maya then asked me, "So, what is our major illusion in our quest for finding the person or entity responsible for any action?

I said, "We know that any action will face a sure death when that on which it depends is removed. A heart operation

44

will not happen if the anesthesiologist is missing, or a cart will not move if the horse is removed. Failing to see the dependence of any action, we fail to perceive the real actors behind those actions. When we wrongly take such actor to be the real cause of an action by ignoring their dependence, we lose the opportunity to have control over the process. What would you say to someone who really tries to whip a cart to move it? If one can easily understand the stupidity and uselessness of whipping a cart, why would one not understand the similar mistake on countless other activities? Unless we have understood the root causes of all actions, we cannot make meaningful decisions for keeping things under control."

Maya asked, "Why do you think we don't know all this already? Don't we have rules, laws and punishments for all the wrongdoers. We do have serious processes to find out the real culprits behind any crime.?"

I said, "We have implemented the laws with the assumption that we are able to get the real actor behind all actions. But do we ever get that real intent behind any action?"

Maya said, "I don't understand."

I said, "It is our illusion to think that when any chain of events in an action ends with a person who might have an intent, we have found the real actor behind the action. In a road accident involving driving under influence of alcohol, we punish the driver who was drunk. From all our discussion today, what do you say about the real actor behind such accidents?"

Maya said, "From what we said, the person held liable for the accident had no intention of the accident. His actions or mis-actions were dependent on the consumption of alcohol, and he wasn't even aware of things happening. In fact, how can he be the root cause when he lacks intent as well as the awareness?"

I said, "But we do punish the human, saying that it was responsible for the accident. We have created the laws for the country based on our limited thinking like the one we apply to a horse and a cart. We have created illusions about the actions and the actors behind those actions. We have failed to understand the driving forces in this universe. We are happy to end our search to the cart-man every time we encounter a similar situation. Unless we understand the root of all actions and the interdependence of activities, we can never control any action in our lives. With the existing laws and rules, we are simply putting a lid over the boiling liquid. If we think we are doing it right with the existing methods and that the laws have taken care of the root cause of the problems, then there shouldn't ever have been any accident because of driving under influence because we already have the laws in place. We have never tried to look at the real driver in any action sequence. If we did, we would have known the right knobs to turn and to end the problems from the root, from the level of the intent."

I said, "We fail to stop petty crimes like theft, burglary or driving under influence on daily basis. When it comes to face the real challenges that affect the whole mankind, we are totally clueless. We can only watch the polar ice melting away, species of animals slowly vanishing from the planet or our lands and oceans getting stuffed with toxic plastic waste. Lacking the intelligence required to find the real cause behind the worsening state of our world, we continue to live in the illusory idea of our control over the things. No doubt, when we stage

46

huge protests to ban the use of single use plastics or have a mass beach cleanup activity, we are doing nothing more than trying to put a lid over the boiling liquid or trying to fight the dragon with nail cutters in our hands."

Maya was listening quietly. A lot was said. It was true. If a solution to a problem was perfect, then the problem would never have recurred. With all the laws in place, we don't see the end to the crimes. We continue to punish the people who are proven beyond doubt to have directly committed the crimes, but there is never an end to the crimes. Maybe we have an illusion about who is the actual driver behind any action. Maybe we are not looking where we should.

I saw Maya write on the whiteboard this famous statement we heard many times.

> *"When the cart does not move, you don't whip the cart."*

5

Objects or Assemblies?

Maya wonders if there was anything that could be called an object? Everywhere one looks, one finds only assemblies.

One Sunday, I thought of fixing an old stool which had its one leg broken for quite some time. It had been with me for more than ten years. During this time, I had already painted it twice and replaced one of its legs. For some reason, I had been attached with its special memories and I was unable to throw it away. While I was trying to shape a log of wood to match with the existing legs of the table, I heard Maya coming from her room. She asked, "Are you sure you want to spend time on fixing it? You could get a new one."

I said, "I can get a new one, but it won't be the same."

Maya said, "Even this one is not the same as itself!"

Her comment made me remember something. I asked, "Have you heard about the Ship of Theseus?"

"A Ship of What?" She asked.

I said, "I think I should tell you about it. You would be surprised how confusing our perception of objects and their identities can be."

Maya seemed ready to listen. I said, "I came to know about it when I saw a movie with the same title. When I was already half-way through the movie and I did not find any mention of a ship, I figured out that the title of the movie didn't mean it in literal sense. That is when I searched online and found the interesting fact about it."

"In short, this is about a fictitious ship of a legendary Greek king named Theseus displayed in a museum. As the time goes on, one of its wooden plank gets rotten and the officers at the museum get it replaced with a new similar plank of wood. The question is raised whether the ship could still be called the Ship of Theseus with one of its parts replaced. As more and more parts of the ship get rotten over time, and get replaced with the new pieces, the question remains whether the ship continues to carry its identity, the *Ship of Theseus*. Eventually a time comes when every single part of the original ship gets replaced. We now have this totally new ship with no remains from the original ship. Can it be called the Ship of Theseus?", I tried to convey the idea in as short as possible.

Maya listened to this very carefully.

She then said, "It is interesting. I don't think we question like this about anything in our daily lives. Our teacher was also saying something like that. She said that our bodies lose many cells on daily basis which continue to get replaced by newer cells. It so happens that in about seven years, most of original cells of our bodies are replaced. Hearing this story from you now makes me think that we all are not different than the Ship of Theseus. We all continue to carry a fixed identity even though our bodies continue to get changed every moment."

"A fixed identity. Very well said. An idea of permanence. Something that doesn't change." I said.

I asked Maya, "Do you think there is anything in reality that doesn't change. Anything that remains the same forever?"

Maya said, "As far as I see, everything changes. It doesn't matter if it changes within a few minutes, hours or in many centuries. There is nothing that we see around which has been forever the same."

I asserted once again, "So it will be correct to say that the reality doesn't remain the same. It is always changing!"

Maya said, "Yes, that's right."

I said, "We are aware that the reality always changes, and yet we expect things not to change. Is this not an illusion? We continue to experience changes within ourselves and others. Yet we continue to behave as if nothing has changed or will change in our lives or in the things around us."

Maya said, "That sure looks like how we behave. Like in the beginning we had what we called as the Ship of Theseus. Then its composition started changing. Though we were constantly aware of the changes going on, we could not let go our idea of its personality or its identity, which feels like a permanent entity."

I asked, "Do you know why the illusion of identity is so strong, that we are not willing to let go the idea of its permanence?"

Maya said, "I am not sure. Why is it so?"

I said, "When we are looking for an identity, a core of something or someone, we are trying to go to its center, the root. We are trying to get hold of that underlying singularity which represents the whole structure uniquely. To make things easier to understand, let's call it the *Self*. The idea in the 'Ship' of Theseus is the idea of the *Self*. The *Self* being the core of the idea of original ship was the reason why its identity was hard to lose when its contents kept on getting replaced. The reason why another ship built with all the original contents cannot be called the Ship of Theseus is because it doesn't have the same *Self*, the underlying singularity that carried the idea of its personality.

Maya asked, "Where exactly can we find this *Self* in anything?"

I said, "The (idea of) the *Self* about any object or a person exists in our minds. It has nothing to do with the thing or the person itself. Any reference to *Self* in someone or something will turn out to be an imaginary concept because there is nothing about it that can be perceived. A *Self* in any object of assembly of objects represents all of its contents in totality (in our minds)."

Maya said, "It seems that you are trying to say that any identity is just an idea. It is an idea of the core of that person of a thing, which we call as the Center, or the *Self*. With no perceptible existence, it seems to exist only in our minds!"

I said, "That is true!"

Maya said, "So this way, whenever we refer to some person or a thing through its identity, we are referring to the underlying idea of permanence, that which is its center or its totality. Is it then, just an idea? An illusory concept?"

"Since nothing in the reality will ever be able to point to the underlying *Self* of anything, you can surely say that!" I replied.

Maya got surprised. She repeated, "What! You mean to say that at its core, any specific person or thing is just an idea? How can we say that? A person is someone we can see, hear, perceive, and experience. It has a physical presence and can act move and influence things physically. How is that an idea?"

I said, "You are confusing between a person and a specific person."

A Self is a permanent entity which does not change, though it may experience changes.

I continued, "When you experience a physical presence through seeing, hearing, touching, smelling or tasting, it is not an illusion, but a reality. But when you take a combination of such physical traits that can be experienced and perceived and then translate the combined perception into an identity, you call it 'A Specific Person'. With that specific person you have created an identity, an illusion of a permanence, its *Self*. Like the one which we called as the Ship of Theseus."

Maya was quiet. She knew I was talking about a subtle difference between reality and an illusion. There was something being perceived, and then there was something being interpreted from those perceptions. A few days ago, she came to know that the reality was being corrupted from what

53

it was to what it was being interpreted as. That corruption was due to limitation of our sense organs to operate in given space and time. Now she was learning that part of the limitation in interpretation of reality was due to our limited ability to comprehend the grand nature of the universe around us.

I tried to explain more. I said, "We know that the reality is always changing. We have trouble comprehending the changes going around us. Things would have been easy if they were fixed because we don't like uncertainties. The creation of an identity is nothing but our quest to know all things from a singular point of permanence, the very core of everything, the *Self*.

"An idea of a personality is one such deep rooted habit in the human mind. A personality, a person, or an identity gives an idea of a permanent entity. A permanent entity is one which does not experience change. All changes happen to it but it does not change. For example, if a person is called James, then James can gain weight and become obese or lose weight to become thin; but he will still be called James. James could be permanently thin, fat or change his body shape over time, but will continue to be known as James. James could be illiterate, and then later attend college to become a graduate, he continues to be known as James. All changes will happen to James, but (the idea of) James will not change. James is nothing but the *Self*, an idea of permanence, a Grand Illusion of a singular permanent entity." I said.

Maya said, "Your explanations look reasonable, but I am not sure if I can totally grasp that a person or a personality is nothing more than an illusion."

I said, "That is all right. We are what we are because of our thousands of years of conditioning. We owe our present manner of perception and interpretation to our language, literature and experiences of all our past generations. If you think you can believe what is being said here even if it doesn't make sense, and go forward, you will be able to appreciate it slowly."

Maya asked, "You spoke of the fictitious story of the Ship of Theseus. Now that you have explained about the idea of the *Self* and the identity of a person or an object, can you explain what exactly is going on with the ship and its identity in that story?"

I said, "Our quest for certainty and permanency in this chaotic world has created a need for an identity or a personality. An identity is nothing more than an idea in our minds. There cannot be any doubt about the Ship of Theseus being affected by replacement of one or all of its parts. It does not matter if the parts being replaced were similar to the original parts or totally different. The ship will still be known and experienced as the Ship of Theseus due to the underlying permanent singularity called the *Self*. If all those original rotten pieces of the original ship were used to create another ship, that new ship will still not be the Ship of Theseus, because of its missing *Self*. Just like James can be thin or fat, but will still be called James, in the same way the Ship of Theseus gets each part replaced with anything else in the world and will still remain – the Ship of Theseus."

"Do you see? The Ship of Theseus is simply the core, an idea. It is the underlying *Self* as a singular permanent entity, independent of the contents of its structure." I said.

Maya asked, "Is this *Self* the core of every perceivable object?!"

I said, "The *Self* is an idea of underlying permanence of the things in our minds. It is a singular and an independent entity; it does not depend on other causes to exist. We have already seen that the existence of James is independent of the behavior or the quality of contents of its body. Would you start looking at James differently if he got a few of his organs replaced by artificial ones? Would you not think he is the same James even if he got his arms or legs replaced with plastic ones? For you, the idea of James' personality is so permanent that no such physical change can influence that. In other words, James is nothing but an expression of the *Self*."

Maya said, "I am not sure if I was able to grasp much."

I said, "I am aware of this. For now, you may just stay with this fact as it is even though it doesn't make sense. As we explore further into the nature of objects, personalities and the universe itself, you will begin to get a feel of it. For now, we can shift our attention to objects."

I then asked Maya, "What do we mean by objects, or things?"

Maya said, "An object is anything that is visible or perceivable and has some form."

I asked her, "Is an object a single individual entity?"

Maya said, "Obviously, an object is a single entity. When we talk of a collection of things, we call them objects."

I asked her, "If there is a group of people assembled for a protest, can it be called an object?"

Maya said, "No. They are multiple people, not a single thing."

I asked her again, "Will they make an object, if I tie them all together so tightly that they cannot move?

Maya made a strange face. "Well, No! Why would you do that?" She said, "They are separate people. Tying them together will not make any difference. No matter how tightly they are bound, they are still a group of people bound together."

I asked, "If there is a large heap of books in the shape of a pyramid, can it be called a single object, the pyramid?"

Maya said, "No. If we see it as a heap of books, we might call them as heaped in a pyramid shape, but will still call them as a collection of books."

I asked her, "If I made a lot of marbles and stick them together to make a big ball, do I have a single object?"

Maya was a bit hesitant. She smiled. She had figured out where I was going with my questions.

She said, "Well, it might possibly be seen as one object, a big ball."

I said, "Do you think, then, an object is also an idea?"

She wasn't expecting that. She asked, "Why do you say that?"

I tried to explain, "Let us assume you enter a museum and see a big shining ball at the entrance. As you come closer, you find out that the ball is actually not a single ball, but an assembly of thousands of glass marbles stuck together in the shape of a ball. What you thought was as a single object a minute ago had been proven wrong. You now see thousands of objects in front of you."

I then asked, "Don't you think the perception of one big ball while entering the museum was simply an idea of one single object?"

Maya said, "It sure seems that the initial perception of a single big ball was an illusion, an idea in the mind."

I asked, "Why do you say that was an illusion?"

Mays said, "Because there was no single object, but a collection of many smaller objects."

Picture 8: We perceive the structure on the left as one big assembly of smaller balls but not as a single object, but the one on the right as single sugar cubes even though both are assemblies of smaller pieces.

I gave her something to question by saying, "Don't we always assume and understand an object to be a single, indivisible entity? Is it right to say that an object cannot be said to be an object, if it can be seen as an assembly of many smaller objects?"

Maya said, "When we commonly refer to an object, we always assume it is a single indivisible entity. A collection of many things seen together is a big mass cannot be called an object."

I said, "So you agree that when we figure out that something is made of more than one objects, then we don't call it an object, but we rather call it an assembly of objects."

Maya said, "Yes, that would be more appropriate."

I said, "Do we ever see anything that is not made of smaller parts? Do we see anything that we should call an object, at least the way we think it is? Is it not impossible to find any single object in this whole universe?"

Maya was surprised. It seems she had not thought thoroughly before agreeing. But it seemed true that as long as things could be broken down into more and more smaller parts, they could not be called as individual objects. All such things would be nothing but assemblies of smaller objects which themselves are again the assemblies of even smaller objects.

I said, "Do you realize that what you see as a vase holding the flowers is not really an object, a single entity? It is an assembly of very tiny particles of clay glued together to give a stable form. In fact, nothing we see around us is actually an object; they are all assemblies."

Maya asked, "Then what actually is the 'Vase' in a vase?"

I said, "The same as what is ship in the *Ship of Theseus*. An idea of singularity, the *Self* that represents the idea of the object."

Maya asked, "So that which we know with as a vase is an idea of singularity, which we may refer to as *Self*? That *Self* which represents everything that a physical vase contains into one single identity?"

I said, "Yes. Our concept of vase as a single object is an illusion. It is an assembly of many smaller parts. When we see it as a single entity, we are referring to its core, the *Self*."

I then asked her, "How did we define our fourth illusion?"

Maya said, "Creating a reality by perceiving one thing for another."

I asked her, "Would you say that the vase is an illusion?"

Maya said, "I understand that a vase is not a single object but a collection of countless other pieces. Yet, I perceive it as a single object instead of an assembly of different smaller objects. It is like creating a different reality by perceiving one thing for another."

I didn't say anything for the moment. I could see that she was not completely convinced how it made any difference knowing that an object is not a single object any more.

As anticipated, she asked, "So what if an object is not a single entity? What's so great in knowing that it is an illusion?"

I asked, "What happens if it falls from the table?"

Maya said, "It breaks, obviously!"

I said, "What do we mean by breaking?"

Maya said, "It breaks! It loses its shape and separates into many smaller pieces."

I said, "Is it the vase which breaks, or is it the illusion that breaks? An illusion that the vase is a single entity. A single entity which cannot and should not lose its present form."

Maya said, "Oh! This is Ridiculous! I never thought about this! Of Course, when something breaks, we feel so bad. We don't want things to be broken or destroyed, especially the ones we like."

I said, "A vase was never a single entity. It was a collection of many pieces. When the vase falls, all the collected pieces fail to keep up their unity and get separated into multiple pieces. There was no vase ever to break anyway."

She asked, "But something still breaks. What is it that breaks?"

I said, "That which breaks is the form. The form which was seen as a vase is not anymore when the vase falls."

I continued, "We imagined a form when there was none. If the vase has a form on the table and loses it as soon as it falls on the ground, then its form is nothing but an illusion. A form that was not only imagined but also thought as a permanent

61

entity. Is this not the first illusion that we had already established?"

Maya said, Yes, we defined our first illusion as imagining form where there is none. First, we mistakenly create a firm identify in shape of a form which does not exist in reality. Then we get hurt when the shape ceases to exist in the way we liked it to exist."

I said, "There is no form in a vase. All there is, is an arrangement of countless smaller pieces in some ordered fashion. This peculiar arrangement which is seen as a form might last for a second or for a few years. Nevertheless, the perceiving of the envelope of the collection as a form is still an illusion. If a large group of people assemble on ground to look like a vase, we will not hesitate to call it an illusion. But we find it hard to call a physical vase an illusion even though we are aware that it is no different than a vase made by a human formation on a ground."

Maya said, "I feel the same way. Even though I can understand that a vase is made of millions of smaller particles, I cannot get rid of the idea of a single object from my mind. Every time a thing we possess breaks, we get affected. We don't seem to overcome our illusion of forms in objects."

I said, "It is understandable. There are two hurdles to be crossed in dealing with the world of illusions. The first one is to know that an illusion exists in place of reality. The second one is to really 'see' the illusion happening. This is difficult to overcome because of limitation of our senses in time and space. We know that the moving picture in a movie or a video is an illusion because it is made of a series of stationary images.

62

Yet, we cannot overcome this illusion because of the limitation of our eyes."

Maya said, "That means it is a good idea to understand the nature of illusions even if it is not possible to break it effects!" Then she wrote on the whiteboard.

If it broke, it was not real.

6

Illusion of Objects

*What are objects? Are objects different than
the properties they exhibit? Do we ever know
an object or is that just an idea?*

One Saturday, I was watching a game of Cricket on the television. It was a five-day test match between India and Australia. Maya came and sat beside me. In about five minutes, she got restless and said, "How can you watch such a boring game for the whole five days?"

I said, "I find it interesting. In fact, there are millions of people like me in the two countries who are glued to their televisions during this tournament season. It is one of the most interesting things to watch."

Maya said, "I don't know. I can't think why people would want to watch such games for so long."

A thought came to my mind hearing her say this. I switched off the television and asked her, "Do you know that each of us views the world in our own way?"

Maya said, "I don't know if it's always true. It may be true for opinions about the things such as this game of Cricket, but

I don't think it might be true for somethings where there cannot be any confusion about it."

I said, "Is it so? Let's try to with some simple example."

Maya said, "Ok. Let's take the case of flowers."

I said to her, "When we talk of flowers, we might imagine that everyone likes them and feels comfortable being around them."

Maya said, "I was going to agree to it, but then I realized that some people do have allergies to pollens. I am sure they would not want to be around some special flowers that they are allergic to."

I said, "That is understandable. If that is the case, I can imagine that the same would happen in case of ice-creams and chocolates too."

Maya said, "Sure. One would find different opinions about chocolates and ice-cremes too. Some would have medical condition about excess sugar while others would have sensitive teeth. As much as most kids would like to eat plenty, there would be some who would have allergies to nuts and would not dare try one of those. I am sure there is no one sure opinion or experience towards any such things."

I said, "People can have different opinion about objects because of their different experiences with them in the past. But if we let go of any opinion, do we still all see the same thing in the same way?"

Maya said, "I don't think so. Take the example of room temperature. The temperature which you find comfortable, mom finds too hot. And what makes mom comfortable, you find it freezing cold. Obviously, you two can never settle on a right temperature around you. A right temperature is not just your opinion. It is your actual perception which is dependent on each of your own physical nature."

I said, "I think this might be true for all the people because each has a unique way of perceiving. Some people have a sharp vision and can see many details in some objects while others might not have a very good vision and would not find the same objects worth appreciating in the same way. Some might enjoy the opera while others might hear it as irritating noise. What appeals to a person as a tasty food smell might repel another because of his intolerance to the smell of a meat."

Maya asked, "Is there really not a single thing that can be 'seen' in the same way by any two people? If there is one thing and everyone looks and feels it differently, where does the problem exist? Is our understanding of the objects incorrect or is our view of the things imperfect?"

I said, "I don't think there might be any issue with our understanding of objects or viewing of them. It could be probably true if we had some illusions about the way we perceive things."

Maya said, "In a way you are right. But I would say that even if our view of the objects is an illusion, we won't know it. Do you remember, you talked about it in the very beginning? You said that what we perceive, is what we think reality is."

I then asked, "But even if we would never know such illusion, is it possible that our understanding of the objects the way we think they are, might be illusory?"

I said, "It must be. Otherwise how do we explain everyone's perspective of the world to be unique and different?"

Maya asked, "How do we find it out?"

I said, "We can find out by exploring it. Let's go over our understanding of the objects again."

Maya said, "But haven't we already gone over it? We had figured out that objects are nothing but assembly of more assemblies."

An object is something that can be perceived. If not perceivable, it can't be an object.

I said, "Yes, we discussed it last and figured out that there is really no substance in the objects. As we go on scrutinizing for their contents, we never find any content there. Nevertheless, something in them ensures that they are still perceivable by our senses."

Maya said, "You are right. In fact, an object is something that can be perceived. If not perceivable, it can't be an object."

I said, "We already know that we perceive by our senses which includes seeing, hearing, touching, tasting or smelling. If we are able to notice some sensation of a sight, touch taste, smell or a sound, we are sure about the presence of an object."

Maya said, "That is right."

I asked, "And what exactly do we perceive when we sense objects?"

Maya said, "I would guess it's the qualities of the objects?"

I said, "Yes. We notice the qualities, or characteristics. We notice the touch of something by noticing its hardness, roughness or softness, or by noticing its hotness or coolness. We notice its shape, color, size and movement when we observe it through our eyes. When we observe sensation in our ears, we notice sharpness, loudness, or softness of its sound. When we taste it, we know if it is hot, cold, sweet, bitter, salty, sour or tasty. When we try to smell, we know about its fragrance. At all times, we are noticing the qualities of an object."

Maya said, "You talked of all inanimate objects. What if we look at a person?"

I said, "It is same for animate as well as inanimate things. When you see a person, you see their appearance, posture, dressing through eyes. You hear their voice and figure out if they sound friendly, threatening or calm. You never know a person really. You only know how their behavior or style is."

Maya said, "Oh! So it's not just about objects; it's about everything and everyone that we perceive through our senses."

I said, "We know about the objects or people through their qualities. While using our senses to perceive them, all that we know about them is their qualities. Can we not simply say that the objects are nothing but their qualities or characteristics?"

Maya said, "What? That makes no sense!"

I said, "I know it seems a radical thought. But think about it; is it not true always? We can try to find as many examples as we can think. And if we find that something is true all the times, can we not make a rule about it, or embrace it as a new habit if it happens to be better than our older habits or traditions?"

Maya said, "I am not sure if I have ever heard anything like this - that objects are nothing but their characteristics. It looks like a philosophical statement that one finds mentioned under the statues, or on the walls or posters which no one cares to give much thought. But I know it very well that no two people look at a thing in the same way, because each person has his own perspective. I believe it would be a good idea to explore if there is a way of observing our world which makes more sense."

I said, "Good! Let's try to frame our proposal. 'An object is nothing but its characteristics'. Do you think a statement like this could also mean that an object is not different than its characteristics?"

Maya said, "Sure. If an object is nothing but its characteristics, then there could not be any difference between an object and its characteristics."

I said, "So, we can say that there is no separation between an object and its characteristics."

Maya said, "True. If an object and its characteristics are the same thing, then there cannot be a separation between the two. "

I then asked, "Does it not mean that it is nothing but an illusion to consider an object detached from its characteristics? Or that an idea that an object can be different from its characteristics is nothing but an imagination?"

Maya said, "Definitely. If we can see that an object is nothing other than its characteristics, then imagining objects and their characteristics as separate is simply an imagination of our minds."

Maya then said, "What you are saying seems like a radical idea. Why do you think that an object and its characteristics are not separate?"

I said, "Are they ever separate?" I paused for a moment. I thought it was the time to start probing this issue with a different way of questioning.

"Is an ice cube always cold?" I asked.

"Yes, it is." Maya replied.

"Is the fire always hot?" I asked.

"Yes," She replied.

I asked, "When you say that the fire is always hot, or the ice is always cold, does it not mean that there is no way ice could be anything but cold, or the fire be anything but hot? Does it not mean that the idea of hotness cannot be separated from the fire, and similarly the idea of coldness cannot be separated from the ice?"

> **An object is nothing but its characteristics or qualities. It is an illusion to see objects detached from their qualities.**

Maya didn't react. She was talking to herself with the words that I just spoke. "Fire is always hot. A fire can never be anything other than being hot. A fire cannot be cold. Fire and hotness. Fire and nothing but the hotness. Fire never without

71

hotness. Fire and hotness, never away, never separate." She kept repeating till she could not see if it would have made any sense to look at the two differently.

I then asked her, "We talked of fire. Do you know what makes you observe and realize something as fire?"

Maya said, "When I see flames emitting reddish glow, I understand it as fire. If it is nearby or if it is far away but huge, I can feel its warmth, or heat too."

I said, "So, you see flames, glow and sense heat and you figure out that it is fire."

Maya said, "Yes, that is right."

I said, "And you said before, that fire is always hot. There is no such thing as cold fire."

Maya said, "True."

I said, "So we really don't know what a fire is. All we know is that it has flames, reddish glow and heat. If there is no heat, there is no fire. If there no flame, there is no fire."

Maya didn't say anything. She was trying to see what I was trying to arrive at.

I said, "All I am trying to say is that we first notice the characteristics, and then create a knowledge of an object. Working up in this sequence we figure out that something that is hot and has reddish glow and flame is known as fire. It is later that we flip our whole sequence of knowing, and solidify this inferred entity as an object exhibiting those characteristics."

Maya said, "What you are trying to say is that we know the objects because we have known its characteristics. According to you, we never knew any object ever in absolute sense. There was no such thing as an object. There were always the characteristics. Are you trying to imply that objects are our illusion?"

I said, "You got it!"

Maya said, "Can we explore more? I don't know if I can believe it."

I looked at the kitchen island. There were some fruits and vegetables in a basked. I said, "Let's look at this onion. Don't we say that the onion has layers or that it is made of layers?"

Maya said, "Yes, this is what we normally say."

I said, "Is it wrong to say that the onion is nothing but the layers?"

Maya said, "No. It perfectly makes sense. If you remove the layers, there is nothing left."

I asked her, "Do you see the difference in the two approaches? When I say that the onion has layers, I am separating the onion from its characteristics of being made of layers. But when I say that onion is nothing but the layers, I see no separation between the onion and its layers."

Maya said, "Let me understand. First, I need to know what you mean by separation between two things."

I said, "Sorry. I will try to go slow."

Maya said, "You said that when we say that the onion has layers, we have separated the onion from its characteristics. I don't understand what is meant by separation. I also don't know why is this separation thing so important to talk about."

I said, "Our way of saying that an onion has layers implies that onion 'contains' layers. What does it mean when you say something contains something? If someone contains something or possesses something, does it not make it possible to lose it too? Not only is it possible to lose it, but also losing it should have no effect on you if there is a separation between you and the thing. If you have a dollar note in your pocket, you might lose it at some point of time. There is physically no effect of the separation of the money from you. You remain the same before and after losing it. Think of another scenario. If a person has cold, he might take some rest and some medicine to get better after some time. Then you will say that the person does not have cold anymore. There is clearly a separation between the person and the cold. If there was not, then the cold and the person would always be inseparable. Our current view of the objects possessing the characteristics clearly indicates that we assume a separation between the two. We fail to realize that every possible accumulation we have at some point of time has the potential to be lost later, because we and our possessions are separate."

Maya said, "I understand what you mean by the idea of separation between the object and its property. You mean to say that we wrongly say that the onion has layers. At no point of time can the onion lose its layers. In fact, one cannot visualize an onion without layers. What you are saying is that if the onion can never possibly lose layers, it is wrong to see it as 'containing' layers. There is no separation between the onion and its layers. An onion is nothing but the layers."

Maya had comprehended what she understood. However, she was not too sure if everything else in the world was as simple as the layers of an onion. She asked, "Don't you think that everyone already knows that onion is nothing but the layers? Can we talk about some other example to check if this generalization is not too simplified?"

I said, "Sure. Let's take another example."

"Let's talk about the birds." I asked, "What do you think comes to your mind when I mention birds?"

Maya said, "Their ability to fly."

I said, "That is right. If I say that I wish to be a bird, you would understand that I am talking about my ability to fly."

Maya nodded.

I said, "Since the only one thing that comes to the mind about the bird is their ability to fly, can we not say that to be a bird is to (be able to) fly?"

Maya said, "I think that still makes sense. Though I am not sure how would this idea cover the birds such as Penguins, that don't and can't fly?"

I said, "Objects or things are nothing but their characteristics. If it can't fly, then it's not a bird! Is that not simple?"

Maya said, "I don't understand. You mean to say that penguins are not the birds because they can't fly! But we all know that Penguins are birds."

I said, "But when I said that I wish I were a bird, do you think there was a chance that I wanted to be like Penguins?"

Maya said, "No. It was clear that you were talking about any bird which could fly."

I said, "Wasn't that easy? If there was only one thing that a bird could relate to, it would be about flying. There is no difference between a bird and idea about its ability to fly."

Maya said, "I think I am getting a feel of what you are trying to say. You are saying that as long as we talk about the things possessing the characteristics, we are looking at them as separate. In the same way as onion is nothing but the layers, the birds are nothing but their ability to fly."

I said, "I don't know why this is not obvious to us anyway? We have already talked about how the objects seem to exist for us. Objects exist because we perceive them. What we perceive is simply the characteristics. If we can only perceive characteristics, then the characteristics (of the objects) are the only reality (for us), not the objects themselves!"

Maya said, "I know! It makes sense. It's just totally opposite to what we are accustomed of. We see the world as made of objects which contain some characteristics. You are saying that one never encounters objects in this universe. All we sense in this universe is the perception of some characteristics. Our mind creates an idea of objects from those characteristics, solidifies this idea and gives it a name. From that point on, it refers to that named object as the real thing possessing all the characteristics that were noticed at its first encounter. A whole flipped way of observation!"

I said, "Yes, it's flipped! There is really no object as a separate entity that has or contains the properties. If there was any, you wouldn't be able to know. Because all you can know is the characteristics or properties. There are properties that you have perceived and created an image of the object based on your perception. Does it explain why everyone has a different perspective of looking at the world and things around us?"

Maya said, "Yes. Because everyone has a unique way of perceiving different sensations of things based on their unique senses, memories and past experiences."

I said, "The memories and past experiences create a conditioning which affects how one perceives objects in future."

I continued, "The process of observation that we are generally accustomed to is not only flipped, but it also contains an idea of separation between the things and their characteristics. This could very well apply to the people and their behavior too. On the other hand, when you start seeing the objects as made up from the combination of its characteristics, you break away the illusion of object being detached from its properties. In reality, there is no such thing as an object detached from its properties or a person detached from his or her habits. It's an idea, an illusion!"

Maya said, "You say that we take objects as detached from its properties in ignorance. I can understand that. We might be unaware that we take the objects as detached from their characteristics. You also say that it is the big illusion which creates a false view of our universe. I don't understand that. What exactly do we do in our lives that makes you say that our idea of separation between people and their habits or object and their characteristics is inappropriate?"

I said, "Let's explore! What happens when we assume that the objects and their characteristics are separate? We already said that with such a point of view, we would not hesitate to try to add or remove some of the characteristics to the objects or people. We think that is allowed because there might be a separation between a person and his behavior, or an object and its properties. In such a possibility, it should be possible to acquire more, or lose some (of properties or qualities) as long as it is just a possession of yours and not really an inseparable part of you. For example, you know that a person and his favorite shirt are separate things. You could ask him to remove his shirt, or make him wear another shirt on top of this without much trouble."

Maya said, "That seems right. If we view one thing as possessing the other then a separation is implied between the two. In such situation it must be possible to add something more or take away what is possessed without disturbing the possessor."

I said, "Don't we try to do similar acts with people and things in our everyday lives? Don't we try to adjust the world around us based on our expectation from different things or people? We want someone to lose a habit or another to gain a new habit as simply as a matter of removing or adding a shirt."

Maya said, "I think I am beginning to sense what is your concern."

I said, "Don't we do it all the time? Is it not like expecting the dogs to stop barking? Or our expectation that our enemy should stop causing disturbance and become friendly with us? Don't we try to control children every few minutes? It is a common sight to see parents trying to stop the children from touching, picking or dropping the things? Do we really expect a world where dogs don't bark, enemies don't hate or toddlers don't play freely? Even if we continue to expect such an illusory world of things following an idea of a particular order, do we really ever achieve such a world? We do achieve such a world, but then those dogs are not really the dogs that the nature created, nor are the children as active and free as the reality gave us. We expect fruits to be devoid of seeds, fishes to lack smell, chickens to be fat and chemicals to kill only the weeds but not the plants. In the process, we continue to play with the nature and continue to separate the things from their inherent properties creating unimaginable damage to us and the nature around us."

I continued, "We do this not only to others but to ourselves too. Have you read motivational books or heard some motivational speakers? How do you think they try to motivate you? Don't you see them asking you to come out of your comfort zone? They ask you to set some goals, follow some process and break the pattern. How do you think they are seeing you in relation to your habits, behaviors or characteristics?"

Maya said, "When they say that one should drop a habit or come out of one's comfort zone, they are thinking that there is a separation between a person and his comfort zone which contains all of his current habits. I am sure it is one thing to ask a person to remove his shoes and a totally different one to make him lose his habit of biting his nails."

I said, "You are correct! You mentioned habits. Do you know what is a habit? Why is it important to talk about it?

Maya said, "A habit is something you do without being aware of it."

I said, "True. Moreover, not only you do it without attention, you do it with perfection and with unlimited energy. You don't get tired doing what you are always used to doing. You can go on and talk to your close friend for hours in your own language and still don't get tired of talking. But when you try to talk to someone in some new language, the one which you are trying to learn, you find it hard to go on for a long time."

Maya said, "I know. I have been studying French language for the last three years, but find it tiresome when I try to talk continuously for even ten minutes. I have to apply a great deal of concentration and find myself drained completely in the process."

I said, "You get tired of talking in the new language because there is a separation between you and the new language. That language has not yet become your part. That has not become your habit. Whereas, when you talk in your mother tongue, there is no separation between you and your language. You and your language are one and the same thing. There is no tiring in you being you."

Maya said, "So, you said that the motivational speakers try to influence people by suggesting them to follow some rules or a system to come out of their comfort zone, their habits!"

I asked her, "Do you now see the illusion?"

Maya said, "I see. When someone is asked to come out of the comfort zone and be motivated to change oneself, it should be understood that it is one of the most difficult expectation. It is like asking one not to be what one is."

I said, "There is another way people assume separation between people and their capabilities. Have you seen experts suggesting or interviewers looking for creativity in terms of out-of-box thinking?"

Maya said, "Yes. People seem to use this a lot. Everyone seems to mention it implying that it is an intelligence worth possessing."

I said, "What is the box in the out-of-box thinking? Is it not true that everyone is already what one is supposed to be at any moment? How can one be more than what one is already unless you imagine a separation between someone and the qualities that person could have? Is it not like asking a parrot to be more parrot than it is? Or asking a dog to be more dog than it is! Otherwise what is out-of-box for a parrot or a dog if not asking outside of what they already are?"

Maya said, "I see your point. To assume that a person could think out-of-box is to assume that a person is capable of being different than his thoughts, capabilities and characteristics. As if he and his thoughts are separate things. That is quite an illusory idea! I see where the gap is in our observation of the worldly objects when you say that our view of them is illusory."

I said, "On top of that, you would hear every commonplace motivator repeating the necessity of positive thinking. They go on telling you to avoid negative thoughts. They assume you are detached from your thoughts. They imagine that you control your thoughts sitting at a distance from them. No. You are not different than your thoughts. You are your thoughts. There is no separation. Whether you call it positive or negative, you are one single entity made of the whole thought process that you maintain. You yourself cannot be the person to control your own thoughts, unless there was a separation."

Maya said, "I am a bit concerned to hear you say this. You say that it is illusory to believe people to be detached from their habits, thoughts or intelligence. Accordingly, you mention that asking people to think out-of-box or trying to motivate them to come out of their comfort zone is a bad idea. Is this not a totally pessimistic view? We do see many examples of people coming out of their comfort zone and achieving success by their hard work."

I said, "You must understand what it means to come out of one's comfort zone. You can only understand it when you are fully aware that there is no separation between oneself and one's comfort zone which contains one's habits, characteristics and qualities. If you are aware that one is not different than one's habit, then you know the amount of hard work that is required if the habit must be removed from one's routine. A habit is not different than you. Do you know how hard it is to remove one's own part? Is it easy for one to cut one's own hands or lose a son in a war? Your hand is your own part, and so is a son to his father. Our comfort zone and our habits are no different. Just hearing an impressive speech by someone or reading a well worded book is not enough to make someone transform. A transformation means complete destruction of the original. To be destroyed is to embrace pain and hardship. We can all talk excitingly about a transformation of a caterpillar to a butterfly, but we cannot imagine the amount of pain and fear it must face at such times."

Maya said, "I get it! I think you are saying that we are not different than our thoughts and our habits. We would not be comfortable making changes to our lifestyle or behavior pattern under normal circumstances unless we face immense challenges that can force us to do so. So, if someone is casually suggesting someone to change or pick a habit, we should be cautious about the lack of sincerity in such public speakers, authors or self-help gurus."

I said, "That is right.

Maya asked me, "Is it easy to break illusions?"

I said, "If only there was a separation between ourselves and our illusions."

I could see her smiling.

Illusion of Separation

*Is there a separation between any two things
in this Universe? Is Individuality nothing
but an Illusion?*

It was summer time and we all had visited a small city in the western region of India. Udaipur is called a city of lakes, and is visited by thousands of visitors every year for its weather, culture and beautiful locations. It had been a few days in the city and we had already visited the palaces, gardens and a few lakes. Today we had planned to visit the local arts museum and were fortunate to be there when a one-hour puppet show featuring the epic sage of Ramayana was about to begin. The string puppets are one of the most popular folk arts of Udaipur, and the local cultural center has been successful in keeping this ancient art alive through promoting the art as well its artists.

We all had sat down in the dimly lit hall with about six rows of chairs. There was a little stage in front covered by the curtains. After a wait of about ten minutes, most of the seats were occupied, and the curtain opened following an announcement. The moment the curtains withdrew, and stage came alive with little puppets hanging by the back curtain

85

depicting different characters such as the king, knights, princes and princesses, horses, demons, birds and snakes. When the show began, a single artist started performing the play of the puppets, controlling their strings artfully, making them walk, run, bend, dance, fight and even make them ride horses. Each puppet was held and controlled by the artist with no more than four strings. Yet, the puppets moved magically when they danced and fought. The artist used different sounds when playing different characters. When the show finished, I asked Maya if she liked the show.

Maya said, "It was one my best experiences. I will not easily forget the fun I had there. The beauty of the whole performance was that there was only one performer, and yet we could experience all the diversity and unique individuality in each character played by those puppets."

I said, "Like an illusion!"

Maya said, "Yes, like an illusion. An illusion of multiplicity when there was none."

Later at home, I started the topic of the puppets again with Maya. I said, "You said something about the illusion of the puppets. Did you really mean it?"

Maya asked, "What? About the illusion of multiplicity? No, I didn't mean it. It was something that came as a conclusion about what happened in the puppet show. When you said that the whole show and its various characters were just the act of a single person, there could not have been a better way to explain it."

I said, "Oh! I thought you understood the illusion which exists in our universe!"

Maya asked, "Which one? Please tell me."

I said, "One where we assume separation between us and all the other living or non-living things in this universe."

Maya asked, "But where is the illusion? Aren't there separate things in this world? How can we say that there are no separate things around when we can clearly see them existing and behaving as separate things?"

I asked, "What do we understand by separation?"

Maya said, "To be separated means to be detached."

I said, "Sure. That seems right. And when we view our worldly existence as detached from each other, we surely assume everything to be having an independent existence."

I then asked to probe her further, "Do we really know what it means to be connected?" What happens when two things are connected? What happens when they are not connected?"

Maya said, "In today's puppet show, all puppets were connected to the artist performing the act. When two things are connected, then one or both might depend on each other. We may say that in such a case, one or both might not have an independent existence. In such an arrangement, if they cease to remain connected, then one or both might lose the purpose for which they were connected."

I said, "You came up with an appropriate example. In a puppet show, both the artist and the puppets were connected through the strings. The puppets will go dead as soon as their connection with the performer is broken. The puppets have life as long as they are connected to the performer."

Then I asked her, "Can we say that the puppets and the artist are not separate?"

Maya said, "Hmm. Having defined this way, I do feel that the puppets and the artist are not separate. It is true that they look detached and have an individuality, but they do have a subtle connection through the strings which makes them interdependent. Without the strings connecting them with each other, they both are lifeless."

I said, "True. The performer and his puppets are not separate in the sense that they don't exist independently. They are different, yet connected, related to each other. They both lose their purpose if the string that connects them is broken. They lose life! The both seem to be a part of a bigger system which contains the performer, the strings and the puppet."

Maya said, "When you mentioned 'bigger system', you meant today's puppet show, right?"

I nodded. The bigger system was the stage on which the puppet show happened today. The artist, the puppets and their interdependence, all was one unified act. It is ignorance, or even an illusion to view them as separate. After all, what remains if we separate them from each other, except for the lifeless puppets and a purposeless artist? On a much bigger scale, our universe is very similar to the puppet's stage. We all seem to be separate but are individually 'connected' to something in the background, subtly controlling our breaths, heart-beats, intuitions and emotions. It was a good time to explore with Maya on the nature of the illusion of separation among us.

Maya interrupted my thoughts. She asked, "I am not sure if things were all that interdependent in today's puppet show. It is right that each puppet was completely dependent on the performer, but were they not completely independent of other puppets?"

I said, "True. In a state of harmony, when everything seems to be operating in a controlled manner, it is not easy to notice the subtle connection between the things. You don't notice any inter-dependence between the puppets because the whole show was being performed by a professional."

Maya said, "I don't understand how the separation or dependence of puppets to each other has anything to do with how good the artist was. After all, each puppet is individually and separately controlled."

I said, "Remember, I said that everything was running smoothly and the artist was an expert. Assume that something happened today which was not anticipated by the artist. For example, let us imagine that one of the strings on one of the puppets broke."

"What do you think might happen?" I asked.

Maya waited before speaking. She said, "It might be hard to imagine what might happen, because I haven't myself ever performed any puppet show. But I can still try to imagine as if I were running the show controlling one puppet with each hand. If one of the strings broke, then it might come as a surprise to me. It might disrupt the continuity and synchronism with which I might have been operating each puppet."

I said, "That's right. Any mishap would certainly break the continuity and the rhythm of the show."

Maya said, "I can think of a similar scenario somewhere else. At times when one of my foot hurts and I can no longer exert full pressure on the hurting leg, I start walking with my other leg taking most of the load. Hardly do I continue doing this adjustment then I find my other leg hurting even more than the original hurting one."

I said, "You mean to say that once a rhythm has broken at one end, you tend to redistribute the attention on all other parts whether or not they were affected."

Maya said, "Yes, this is how everything seems to work. When a part has become weaker, the other stronger part starts taking up more load than it usually takes."

I asked her, "So, what do you think the puppet artist do when one of the strings on one of the puppets break during the show?"

Maya said, "While everything was going on normally, he would be effortlessly going on doing his show as usual. But as soon as one of the puppet faces challenge, he must divert more of his attention and effort on the affected puppet, because it won't behave as it usually does. He might either have to move his fingers more, or bend his hands less, or do some improvisation with his voice so as to cover up the accident such as the puppet exhibiting the pain. Whatever he does,

90

would be totally unpredictable and he wouldn't be prepared for it."

I saw that Maya had picked up the fine details. I waited for her to tell more.

Maya continued, "As he would prepare himself to put more attention on one affected puppet, he must inadvertently lose some of his attention on the other puppets which he controls from the other hand."

I said, "So the broken string on one puppet makes the performance of the other puppet get affected, just like your healthy foot feeling pressured when the other foot gets hurt."

Maya said, "Exactly!"

I said, "It means that as long as things are working normally, and everything is in harmony, you don't see that things are interconnected. In such a state of harmony, the illusion of separation in things appear and it feels as if people and things have an independent existence. As soon as some disturbance happens in one corner, and everything else .gets shaken up to compensate for the change noticed."

Maya asked, "Do we notice anything like this in our lives?"

I said, "We all breathe the same air. What you exhale is taken in as someone else's breath. The oxygen we need is provided by the trees and plants, while we give out the carbon dioxide needed by the trees. All the creatures and the vegetation on this planet form a closely connected system through our breath."

I continued, "We are aware of our sharing and exchange of common resources like earth, water and air but we do not pay much attention to this integrated life of ours. Under normal circumstance, you go to school in a bus, take subways to visit different places in the city, walk in the busy market and do shopping in a crowded place without any special consideration. But, if you happen to hear of a virus threat, you immediately become cautious of public exposure. You take care not to come too close to others. Despite your avoiding contact or an exposure, it's possible that you catch an infection through somewhere you don't know."

Maya said, "Yes. I am aware of this. We don't mind our regular exchange of air through breathing, unless that air happens to be contaminated through smoke, bad smell or some sort of infection. It seems we do know about our integrated life only in terms of harmful effects. As long as things are going in normal way, we feel we have an independent existence."

I asked Maya, "Do you know how it affects the world when you have an illusion of separate existence?"

Maya was quiet. She wanted to hear what I had to say.

I continued, "When you hear a news article on global warming and the reducing ice on poles, you don't worry. When you see miles of ocean covered in plastic trash and rubble, you don't worry. When you are made aware of the amount of plastic toxicity found in the bodies of aquatic animals which leads to their suffocation or death, you don't worry. When you are told about the reducing water in the rivers, species on the verge of extinction or the reduction in the number of bees, you don't worry. You don't care about anything happening around you because you think of your existence as separate and independent from everything around you. And when do you know that you are not separate? You know it when the tragedy arrives, and you have no longer sufficient water to drink, or sufficient crops to feed the animals and humans. You know when it is already too late to correct anything."

Maya said, "What you are saying is that not only we are leading our lives in illusions but are hurting ourselves a great deal due to this ignorance about our illusory separation from everything else in this universe!"

I said, "Yes. Our ignorance and our illusions are costing us a great deal."

I suddenly remembered something. It was the play of puppets that started this thought about our illusion of separation. In the sense that we all share some common resources like the threads of the puppets, we were able to visualize the balance and synchronism that tends to exist among all things and the environment. But there is another quite a different way of looking at things too. A way which looks at the kind of stuff we are made of; our core content.

I asked Maya, "When we were talking about the idea of separation, we figured out that things cannot be said to be separate if there exists any kind of connection between them. Let's think of a different scenario. When it is raining, and all water drops in the air are distinctly detached from each other, would you call them separate? Is there any connection between them? Are the drops related to each other?"

Maya said, "They don't seem to have any connection, and they are totally separate. Yet, I think they might be related to each other."

I asked her, "What makes them related to each other?"

Maya said, "They all are the same! They have exactly the same content within them."

I probed her further, "What happens when they have the same contents?"

Maya said, "When they are same, then they react to everything in the same way. When it is hot, they all vaporize. When it is cold, they all freeze. What happens with one, happens with others too in exactly the same way. It is true that there is no physical connection between the two drops of water, but they all have the same behavior."

I said, "You are saying that a common content between the two things can be seen as the connection between two otherwise separate entities."

Maya said, "I think so. Their common contents work as the connection between them."

I said, "You said something interesting. Two totally separate entities may still be related and connected due to their sharing of some common characteristics. It is like two different objects having some amount of iron in them. They both will get attracted to a magnet in the same way. The two pieces have no physical connection, yet they exhibit the same behavior to a particular action. They can't be called separate based only on their physical separation."

Maya said, "I remember something like this. When we went to the Legoland, what I found interesting was that there were miniature cities, buildings, cars, cranes, and humans which were all built using small blocks made of plastic."

I said, "You mean to say that even though everything looked and behaved like a miniature version of our universe, it was actually nothing but little pieces of plastic."

Maya said, "Yes. Every moving or non-moving thing there was simply a piece of plastic. No matter how differently it's role was defined in those presentations, but at its core it was not different from any other piece that miniature city."

I said, "So, you are trying to say that since they all were composed of the same material, they could easily swap their parts and change the look of their world. What was a hand of a toy policeman, might easily become a window shelf in one of the buildings when they change its look next time."

Maya said, "Yes. This is what I am trying to say. When we all are made of the same stuff which can be and does recycle in the nature, we cannot be said to have a separate and an independent existence."

I was listening to her quietly. There was nothing to be said.

Illusion of Knowledge

*Our idea of knowledge is an illusion, and
our idea that such knowledge leads to
intelligence is even a bigger illusion.*

I came home to find Maya looking at a video with great
interest. When she saw me entering the room, she paused the
video and asked me with excitement, "Have you seen this?
They have this five-year-old in their studios and the child
seems to know so much! He can identify all the countries, their
flags, currencies and a lot more!"

I said, "I am not sure about this particular one, but I have
seen it many times in the news articles or television programs
where some kid is shown to possess a high intelligence. In my
view, these kids are made to memorize a lot of information by
their parents who themselves have a limited idea about
memory, knowledge and intelligence."

Maya was surprised by my 'negative' statement. She said,
"I thought you would be impressed. In fact, I was myself
astonished at the child's ability to remember so much at such
an early age! I am shocked that you don't find the little kid's
knowledge about our world impressive! Moreover, I am not

sure if I would agree that you don't find knowing a lot about our world as a sign of knowledge and intelligence."

I said, "I know, it seems impressive to see a child able to memorize so much while we have to struggle trying to remember what we are taught in the school. What I am trying to say is that we might be having very wrong ideas about what knowledge and intelligence is."

Maya said, "Let me guess. Are you trying to say that knowledge and intelligence are illusions too?"

I said, "Not the knowledge and intelligence as such, but our perception about the knowledge and intelligence. That is surely an illusion!"

Maya said, "I was quick to make my opinion about what you said about the child in the video. But if our ideas about the knowledge and intelligence are illusory the I would want to understand what is wrong with the way we currently acquire and evaluate them in ourselves and others."

I saw that she was interested in hearing how our current views on the issue of knowledge or intelligence were not realistic. I asked her, "Should we start by our present understanding of the words, knowledge and intelligence?"

Maya said, "That will be a good idea. Let me quickly see what the dictionary.com says about these words."

I smiled. I saw that the shelf in front of us had stacked about half a dozen of different dictionaries. Yet, it had become a hassle to go and pick one of them and flip its pages to find the information of interest every time. It had become easier for us to tap a few keys on our phones or computers to get the solutions to our queries. I saw that Maya had opened a webpage showing the different meanings of the word which looked like this.

knowledge

noun

1. Acquaintance with facts, truth or principles ..
2. Familiarity or conversance ..
3. Perception of fact or truth ..
4. Awareness

...

I said, "Can we say that by knowledge we mean acquaintance, familiarity, perception or simply awareness of facts, truth or principles?"

Maya said, "That looks reasonable."

I asked her, "Do you see the difference between all of these?"

Maya asked, "You mean between acquaintance, perception and awareness?"

I nodded.

She was not sure. She was waiting for me to speak up.

I asked, "What do we mean by acquaintance? How to we become acquainted with something? What happens when we become acquainted by something?"

Maya said, "I do have an idea about it, but I am sure you want to lead me somewhere very specific. I would let you speak."

I said, "Fair enough! First, to be acquainted or familiar with something, you need something. There cannot exist an idea of acquaintance or familiarity by itself. When I say to you that I am familiar, I won't be making sense. You would be expecting me to say more, so that you know what I am familiar about."

Maya said, "That is right. Are you indicating that familiarity or acquaintance is a dependent activity?"

I said, "Yes. An idea of a knowledge as acquaintance or familiarity with the people or things in this world is dependent on the existence of those things. There is no knowledge by itself which you would understand as acquaintance."

Maya asked, "I do remember we talked about dependency in terms of finding the real actor behind an action. I understand that any action that depends on some other causes is really not an action, it is more like a response. However, I don't understand why we should be concerned if a knowledge of something is dependent on something else."

I said, "That is a very good question. Let me ask you this. What would you think if you see me watering the weeds in my yard?"

Maya said, "I would think that to be a very senseless thing to do. Why would someone water the weeds, instead of getting rid of them?"

I said, "This is right. Your current knowledge about this act is dependent on all that is known to you at this moment.

You know that watering a plant is a good thing because it makes them grow. You also know that weeds are undesirable plants and they should not be allowed to grow. So, your current knowledge used all the information to form an intelligent observation to figure out that I was doing a senseless act."

Maya said, "Yes. That is true."

I said, "What if I said that I was watering the weeds so that it became easier to pull them off the ground along with the roots? This would make the process of eliminating them more efficient."

Maya got surprised! She said, "Wow! I didn't see that coming. It was not a senseless thing to do, but a very intelligent act."

I said, "The very fact that a knowledge has to depend on other facts, makes it incomplete. Any new piece of information will make the existing knowledge obsolete. The act which seemed stupid turned out to be a wise one when we added another piece of information.

Maya agreed.

I said, "Let's take another example. We all know feeding the hungry is a good deed. It shows our sympathy for other lives."

Maya said, "Yes. It is seen as a kind act."

I said, "Would you say the same when a farmer is feeding his chickens for a few weeks?"

Maya said, "Oh, no. He doesn't have any sympathy for their lives or good intentions towards them. He feeds them so that they grow big enough to be sold and fed to others to make money."

I said, "There you go! I hope we can agree on two things. First, no knowledge is ever complete, because any new information can change the existing knowledge. Second, the knowledge that depends on other factors can never be the source of intelligence.

Maya said, "I think I will have to agree with you."

I said, "We can see how the knowledge gets created about anything in this world. Let's say you met with a person named Tom today. You would say that there was no knowledge of Tom before you met him, as you had no acquaintance or familiarity with him. Once you have met him, you remember his name and his looks in your brain. Next time when you meet him again, you would say that you know Tom. This would mean that you remember similar appearance from your memory and you can also recall the name associated with that appearance. This way of knowing, when you are acquainted with a person or a thing depends on your use of the memory."

Maya said, "You are saying that the one way we understand knowledge as an acquaintance with facts, truth or principles needs the facts, truth, principles as well as their past memory to know them."

I said, "Yes. This is the knowledge that the child in the video is exhibiting. He has been made familiar with a lot of things from our world. His knowledge is his familiarity with all the information that was made available to him in the past. The thing that surprises us is the amount of information that the child has been able to store in his memory as well as his ability to reproduce such data when inquired."

Maya asked, "Are you trying to suggest that the behavior the boy is exhibiting has nothing to do with knowledge? Is knowledge really not an acquaintance with the facts?"

I said, "This is part of I am trying to tell. As of now we have seen that our present interpretation of knowledge is dependent on the objects of knowledge as well as memory. Such a knowledge is an illusion, not a true knowledge. We can easily establish that knowledge does not have to depend on any object. The true knowledge is nothing but a state of awareness. All objects of knowledge surely depend on the awareness or the perception of them, but the awareness or the knowledge does not have to depend on the objects."

Maya said, "I never heard anything like that before. But I am sure I can wait to hear what you have to say."

I said, "It is not just about the object, but even the knowledge which depends on memory is not true knowledge. It is simply a mechanism of repeating something known from the past. The true knowledge does not depend on the memory. Any knowledge based on memory is inferior to a knowledge without a memory."

Maya seemed surprised. She said, "Wow! I don't believe it. Are you saying a person who does not remember anything is far more knowledgeable?"

I said, "No. I am saying that a person devoid of any memory is far more receptive to the knowledge compared to someone who already has a knowledge about current observation."

Maya asked, "Why is the knowledge without a memory better than a knowledge with a memory? From what you say, it seems that being receptive to knowledge is a sign of a better knowledgeable or an intelligent person."

I said, "If you have already known something, then on the next encounter with a similar object, your observation is never comprehensive or complete. Your future observations are partial, relative to the previous observations. This is the reason that such a knowledge which is clouded by the past memory and experience is not receptive to the knowledge in its entirety."

Maya said, "You mean to say that an observation with memory is only about the differences from the previous observations?"

I said, "Yes. When you observe something that you have known in the past, all you see is the change from the past. You never see any fact with fresh eyes if you have some knowledge about it from the past. In comparison to this, a person with no knowledge of the past observes with total and complete attention."

Maya said, "That makes sense. I can understand why a knowledge with memory must be called inferior to a knowledge without memory. It seems any kind of dependence whether on objects of knowledge or memory of past observation limits fresh acquisition of knowledge."

I said, "This is right. As long as there is a dependence, there is no fresh knowledge."

I asked Maya, "Tell me one thing. What goes through your mind when you see a child showing extra-ordinary capacity to remember so much information?"

Maya said, "We think that the child is very intelligent."

I said, "I thought so. It seems we all understand that intelligence is dependent on the knowledge which is dependent on the acquaintance with lot of things which is dependent on our ability to remember them."

Maya said, "So, not only is our idea about knowledge inappropriate, our interpretation of intelligence too is wrong because it depends on the knowledge in presence of memory.

I said, "That seems right. There is another thing that bothers me besides this idea of associating memory with intelligence. It seems that we think that the knowledge and therefore, the intelligence is an individual's possession. In our schools and colleges, we treat every student independent of other students and evaluate their knowledge on individual basis. Each student is given a separate test and is graded on his or her ability to remember and apply all that had been perceived, understood and remembered by them in the past. It is like we view every person capable of being a complete entity with his or her share of knowledge."

Maya said, "Yes. When we talk about knowledge or intelligence for humans, we usually care about individual knowledge. When we must think of the examples of high intelligence, we tend to remember individuals like Einstein or

Edison. We never say a particular group of humans was highly intelligent except for some occasional reference of the intelligence of a group, community or humanity in a general sense."

I said, "We might talk about the intelligence of a group, race or the humanity, but we are focused on individuals all the time. When a person completes his or her individual education and training, the job interview process evaluates a person as a separate entity. Those who evaluate a person's capacity to work as a team are also trying to judge it as an individual's skills to adjust with others. Once in the job, every single person is responsible for one's own skills and abilities to operate either individually or in group. Thereafter, the performance evaluation and the career growth are directly dependent on the person's individual intelligence, capabilities and personal contribution towards the overall success of the team or the company."

Maya said, "I see. Yes, when we talk about knowledge or intelligence, we understand that each one of us has an unlimited capacity to possess such qualities individually, and we do not ever consider measuring or utilizing the intelligence or the knowledge of a team of a few members on the whole."

I said, "So, we all think that knowledge is an individual capacity to memorize, recall and apply information as needed."

Maya said, "I think that is true. And we treat intelligence as an individual idea too. When we talk about the intelligence in other species such as ants or bees, we identify their intelligence as swarm intelligence."

106

I asked, "Imagine you are a manager of a company which intends to hire a few smart and intelligent people to develop intelligent machines. You expect the employees to possess abilities to process great amount of data as well as making quick decisions. Do you select individuals who show both memory and speed capabilities or do you select a person who shows even one of such traits?"

Maya said, "If I were the hiring manager who expects the employees to be capable of handling large amount of data as well as possessing quickness of mind, then I will not settle for someone with only one of the skills. After all, what good is a person who is able to remember a lot of information but cannot analyze and utilize that data as quick as needed for the task, especially if that is one of the essential requirements!"

I said, "I know. It is because we treat every person as a complete individual isolated from others. Therefore, we treat intelligence also centered individually in each person separately. However, this is not how we really operate with other things not involving humans. We do see the colony or ants or group of bees making intelligent decisions. But we ignore such much superior examples of intelligence around us in our ignorance. We continue to look intelligence and knowledge in each individual separately even though we could achieve far more intelligence if we did not separate the intelligence based on each individual separately."

Maya said, "I don't understand what you are saying."

I said, "Let's forget the interview process for some time. Assume that you are designing an intelligent machine. You intend to achieve the required intelligence by putting a large memory and a high-speed processing part. You look in the market for the right kind of pieces which would meet your memory and processing capacity. You find a part which can handle huge memory, and another part which can process data at a very high speed. You use the two parts and design your machine."

Maya said, "Ok. What are you trying to say?"

I said, "You didn't notice! Did I try to find a single part which could handle both memory as well as the speed? Does it matter if I use two different parts, each of which can handle one thing best? In the end, all I want is a big machine capable of handling lot of data at a high speed."

Maya said, "I get it! You mean to say that when it comes to humans, we tend to see them as a complete entity capable of possessing all the intelligence as desired. But when it comes to non-humans, we don't mind combining several of them to observe the intelligence whether it happens to be the ants, bees or the parts of a machine."

I asked, "Let me ask you again now. When you invite candidates for the interview, would you want to be specific about every person capable of possessing high memory as well as high speed or would you be intelligent enough to look at the bigger picture and select a candidate even with one unique capacity?"

Maya said, "Obviously. When I can design a machine with two different parts, one for memory and other for speed, why can I not work with two employees, one of those being smart about handling huge data and the other being quick about taking intelligent decision? I am sure, the two working in unison would create an intelligence rarely seen in any one individual."

I said, "So, you do see that our view of imagining intelligence as an individual trait is faulty, or simply illusory! We spend all our life looking for intelligence limited to individuals. When we find the examples of collective intelligence of groups, we do not get a message that our system of education, training, hiring and incentivizing individuals based on their individual capacity is making us miss the source of a bigger intelligence."

Maya nodded. She could see that we as humanity never gave any consideration to the idea that when it comes to intelligence, the individuality has no meaning. This idea of division in the concept of intelligence is as illusory as the idea of dividing the continuous unbroken reality into separate divisions in space and time. With such ignorance, we go on carrying our strange ideas about the supremacy of individual's capacity of memorizing huge details of the past and current affairs.

I asked Maya, "Besides our idea of intelligence being restricted to the humans on an individual basis, do you see a problem with our approach of utilizing memory as a tool to apply knowledge and create intelligent solutions?"

Maya said, "I am afraid, I don't."

I said, "Let us first check what does a dictionary say about intelligence."

Maya referred to the dictionary. She said that according to the dictionary, intelligence meant a capacity for learning, reasoning, understanding, or similar forms of mental activity.

It simply meant that intelligence was an ability to utilize the knowledge. It became even more important to understand our inherent flaws in understanding what knowledge truly was, because unless we possessed right knowledge, we couldn't possibly have proper intelligence.

I said, "According to the dictionary, intelligence is a capacity of performing mental activities which include learning, reasoning, or understanding. Let us talk about each of these mental activities."

I asked her, "What do we mean by mental capacity?"

Maya said, "I would think of mental capacity to be about one's ability to store information as well as to be able to recall it when needed for an action in future."

I said, "So, you are trying to say that a person with a higher capacity for mental activity should be one who can remember and apply different kinds of information. This is what we all generally understand by intelligence.

Maya waited for me to say more.

I continued, "Let us imagine a situation where a little boy goes for a stroll in its village with an empty bag. As you know children are curious and get interested in anything that attracts their attention. As the boy walks through the streets and the farms, he encounters various objects, which he picks up and puts in the bag with great joy. Within no time his bag is full of different kind of things such as fruits, flowers, bottles, cans, toffee wrappers, seeds, and leaves."

I asked Maya, "Can you use your imagination and visualize what happens as the time goes and the boy continues to wander in the village looking for his treasure?"

Maya said, "When the boy started, his bag was empty. It would have been easy to carry the bag in the beginning because the bag was light. As the boy continues to fill it with different things, the bag must become heavier. I think this will impact his ability to continue doing what he had been doing. Not only will the bag become heavier, it will also continue to have less free space with every new thing dropped in it."

I asked, "What do you mean when you say that the boy cannot continue to do what he had been doing?"

Maya said, "In the beginning the boy was picking up anything and everything that he found interesting because the bag was empty and light. Later when there is a limited space in the bag, the boy needs to make a choice between picking or dropping any new object he finds. He will also find it difficult to walk as fast as he was walking before, because he has to carry more weight with every new thing picked on the way."

I said, "So, you are saying that as the bag is getting filled more and more, the child is becoming more slower and more cautious about storing any new thing it finds. This means that not only does it affect the capacity to fill new objects in the bag, but also the speed with which he could observe an object and store in its bag. He needs to pause, think, and decide if the object is worth picking and storing."

Maya asked, "At such times, would it not be easier, if the boy emptied the bag of the things that are not as good as the new thing it found?

111

I said, "Would you expect a child to throw away a treasure that it has collected?"

Maya said, "No way! It was just a random thought. That wouldn't work."

I asked, "Now tell me, what method does the boy use when trying to decide if he needs the new thing it found, especially when the bag is heavy and has a limited space?"

Maya said, "If I were in such a situation, I would ask myself if I had already picked up a similar thing, or a thing that served a similar purpose as the new thing being picked. If it was a flower, I would decide if I needed another flower in my bag if I already had picked five flowers before."

I said, "You mean to say that when you have a heavier bag and a limited capacity, you would look at the new things and make a decision about them based on what you have already collected in your bag."

Maya said, "That is right. If my bag was empty, I would not have tried to make such a decision."

I said, "This means that there was a difference in the way the boy was observing things when his bag was empty compared to when his bag was getting filled up. In the beginning, the boy was picking up things as they seemed interesting, and later he was cautious about the way it was looking at them. He was moving slower and spending his time comparing the objects based on their size, weight, and with the things already collected in past."

Maya asked, "What is this story of the child about?"

I said, "Our brains work no different than the child of our story. The little boy going out with an empty bag is analogous to a fresh mind with no concepts and ideas. In the beginning, each one of us has a mind which is empty, devoid of information of various kinds such as names, forms, processes and experiences collected from past. As we move in this world, we encounter various things, ideas and experiences, which we store in our memories. As we continue to learn in the schools, colleges, homes, offices and all other places, we go on adding those memories and experiences to our brain. This ever-increasing storage is like the child's bag which becomes heavier with the acquired knowledge and built-up concepts about various things based on our personal experiences. This affects our capacity to grasp new ideas, concepts or knowledge because not only does the mind becomes slower, but it also has to decide whether or not to accept it. The acceptance of new knowledge becomes increasingly difficult because of the possible conflict with the already acquired knowledge."

Maya said, "Wow! This is ridiculously strange!"

I knew she had got the idea of the paradox. But I wanted her to say it herself. I asked, "What is so strange?"

Maya said, "The fact that the more knowledge you acquire, the less new knowledge you will collect. The intelligence, as we understand is the capacity to learn, reason and understand. If we believe that the more knowledge should make us intelligent, then we are contradicting with the way the mind works, which actually becomes more and more lazy and unable to accept new knowledge because it is already occupied with previous knowledge, concept and information."

113

I said, "Would you say that the idea that more knowledge leads to more intelligence is unrealistic, or illusory?"

Maya said, "Sure, it seems so."

I said, "Remember it was only the first part of the definition of intelligence which mentioned about capacity of mental activity as one indicator of intelligence. It also mentioned about a capacity of reasoning and understanding. Do you know what is involved in reasoning and understanding?"

Maya said, "I think one needs to have information already available in the mind to logically deduce, reason, analyze or understand something.

I said, "You are right. To understand something new, you need to have known something already, with which you compare the new knowledge. Do you know what it means?"

Maya said, "I am not sure."

I said, "If I want to show you a new process, product or an idea, I cannot make you grasp it unless I make it easier for you to compare it with something you already know. If I want to introduce you to a new religion, you would try to understand in terms of the one you already know. If I show you a new building, lake city, mountain or a stadium, you will compare it with your existing knowledge of those structures. Only when you have not had a previous experience with something new being introduced, you will understand something completely because you stop 'trying' to understand in such times."

Maya said, "I don't understand. How can you understand something completely when you stop trying to understand?"

I said, "When you try to understand something, you compare it with previously known thing or a fact. In this process, all you record is the difference between the two. You never know or understand anything completely because you always try to understand it by means of comparison. But when you encounter something totally new, you don't try to understand or compare. You just observe, experience and absorb it as it is. This fresh encounter is the only true knowledge you get when you get to experience something for the first time. In all future encounters, you are unable to look at things with a fresh mind."

Maya said, "This actually means that the more we know the world, the lesser we understand all further encounters with the world. This too means that we actually become dumber and dumber because we cannot freshly understand anything due to our previous knowledge of them!"

I said, "I am afraid that is so."

I continued, "Likewise, the mental activity of reasoning also involves trying to analyze a situation. One would only be able to analyze something when one has some previous experience with issue at hand. One cannot reason if one has no data to prove or disprove a fact. This means that one is limited to reason an issue only to the limit of one's own previous exposures to the related facts. You can say that the reason a fish will use will not be suitable for a frog or a lizard. Even if we limit ourselves to the fish, we can say the same thing about inability of a fresh-water fish to reason with a salt-water fish."

Maya asked, "Do you mean to say that the (existing) knowledge has no relation to the intelligence in reasoning?"

I said, "Yes. If an atheist tries to argue with a person believing in Christianity, it won't be possible for anyone to understand each other's point of view. Both will fail to understand each other's reasoning because of the lack of sufficient information in their minds about the other person's point of view."

Maya said, "That is so true. I see in my school an ever-going debate between two sections of students, those following the left- wing against the right-wing thoughts. I never ever see any single time when a good reasoning by one seems to make way to the other side's mind and that they actually understand the opposite point of view."

I said, "It seems we talked over the capacity of learning, reasoning and understanding in relation to the knowledge, which is nothing but the storage of all collected information from the past. We should be able to discard the prevalent view that intelligence should be dependent on amount of knowledge in terms of memory accumulated by someone."

Maya was quiet for a moment. She heard me saying that accumulation of more knowledge leads to a lesser capacity to know more. She asked, "Is there a way out?"

I asked, "Are you asking what the way to unlimited knowledge is?"

Maya nodded.

I said, "Go back to our story of the little boy who is out in the village on a treasure hunt. Is there a way that he is not limited in his quest to look, pick and drop it in his bag by the constraints of weight and the size of the bag?"

116

Maya said, "The only way it could work is when there was a hole in the bag."

I said, "There you go!"

Maya was surprised. She said, "What! I don't get it!"

I said, "As you said, if there is a hole in the bag, the bag will not be able to hold the things and they will keep getting slipped out of the bag. The boy will continue to pick and store every new thing he finds in his excitement and will never be constrained by a heavier bag or not much space left in the bag. In the same way, if one does not pay much attention to the past experiences and emotions and continues to explore the life as it comes, one will never be exhausted and constrained by the weight of the memory to learn and know fresh knowledge."

Maya said, "You made it sound so simple. I wish we all were that simple to drop everything from our memories as soon as it served its purpose. When you said in the beginning that you were not impressed by the video of the child's ability to memorize, I was not comfortable. I thought you were being cynical. I was clueless how limited we have been in our understanding of the basic of knowledge, understanding and intelligence. We all continue to live with the idea that memory is knowledge."

I said, "There is yet another misconception that we use excessively about knowledge."

Maya asked, "What is that?"

I said, "We think that the knowledge is something that can be quantified. The quantification helps in measuring and comparing two individuals to rank them according to their different level of knowledge. It makes sense for us to measure the 'amount' of knowledge because that helps us to rationalize differential rewards to individuals performing different jobs in the society."

Maya said, "Why do you say that the knowledge is not a quantifiable thing?"

I said, "I think that is a wrong question. This question is based on one of the illusions that we ourselves created."

Maya asked, "Which one? One where you said that we first created imaginary shapes and then later try to fit every observed reality according to them?"

I said, "Yes. By asking why the knowledge must not be quantified, you are assuming that everything must be capable of being measured and quantified. I don't blame this thinking. There is no way the mind can operate outside the realm of measurement and comparison. It needs to fit everything that it notices into some set of rules, definitions or an understanding that it already knows about."

Maya said, "I think I see what you are trying to say. You are saying that we cannot escape from our habits of measuring and comparing anything we notice. Being slaves of habitual tendencies of own minds, we continue to do this even with those things that cannot be measured or compared. To assume that knowledge could be quantified is far from reality."

I said, "You are right. There is no truth in the idea of perception or knowing being less or more in terms of quantity. You either perceive or you don't. You are either aware or you are not. To develop an idea about how aware one is compared to another is just an imagination. The knowledge as acquired through senses of awareness just exists, with no concept about how much or how little."

"I am not sure about this," Maya said.

I asked her, "We can explore this right now. Do you know what is two multiplied by twelve?"

Maya said, "Yes. It is twenty-four."

I asked, "Do you know what the square root of thirteen is?"

Maya said, "I don't know."

I asked her, "Do you know that you don't know the answer to this question?"

Maya said, "Yes. I know that I don't know (how much square root of thirteen is)."

I said, "So you still know (something)!"

Maya was quiet. Of course, she knew. She knew that there were some things that she knew as well as many other things that she didn't know. But in all the cases, she knew. She knew because she was a piece of life with awareness. As a sentient being, she had this wonderful gift of knowledge which was not dependent on anything other than itself. As long as she was aware, she 'knew'. It is only when she lost consciousness, or went to sleep, she wouldn't know (that she didn't know).

"You either know, or you don't," Maya smiled.

I knew why she smiled. How could someone know a little or a lot! A complete knowledge must mean that every single piece of information is known. As long as someone has a knowledge with limited information, the acquisition of new piece of information changes the knowledge completely. Since it is never possible to have all the knowledge available, a total knowledge is a fallacy.

I asked her, "Do you know who an intelligent person is?"

She didn't reply. She knew I was going to tell her anyway.

I said, "One who knows his or her stupidity."

I could see her pondering on this statement.

After some time, she asked me, "Do we not quantify intelligence too? Is it equally absurd to do so?"

I said, "You are right. Just like knowledge, we also seem to quantify intelligence. In fact, we have a measure of intelligence known as IQ. We believe that the ability of someone to solve several standard format questions within certain time is a direct indicator of amount of intelligence in that person. The results of such tests are summarized as a numeric value known as IQ."

Maya asked, "Do you mean to say that the more a person answers such questions in a given time, the higher is the IQ?"

I said, "Yes, we believe that besides possessing a lot of knowledge, an intelligence is also a matter of how quickly one can solve problems and arrive at best solutions."

Maya asked, "Do you think that is not correct? Why should someone not be called intelligent if he or she knows a lot of things or can solve tricky problems in a very little time?"

I said, "What has the time duration to do with intelligence? Just like knowledge, one is either intelligent or one is not."

Maya said, "I don't get it."

I asked her, "Let us go over a scenario. Imagine that three people are imprisoned for an indefinite period in three separate rooms on an island which are similar in every respect. They all try their best to escape and return to their homes. One person is able to break and run away within a week. Another person also manages to run away successfully after a month. The third person keeps on trying but can never escape. What would you say about their intelligence?"

Maya thought for some time and then said, "I believe that one who manages to break and run away successfully is intelligent while the one who cannot escape is not. He is not intelligent because he is unable to figure out a way to escape and we already know that there exists more than one way to break the prison and free himself. However, we cannot compare the intelligence of the first two prisoners just by looking at the amount of time they took to solve a problem. There could be many reasons for one person arriving at a solution earlier than the other. One who took more time might be a perfectionist and would want to analyze several scenarios to confirm his solutions for their accuracy, validity or repeatability. I don't think that the time to solve a problem is necessarily an accurate indicator of one's intelligence."

I said, "I think so too. But we use the time as a means to differentiate people about their intelligence all the time. When we take the tests, we give everybody the same question paper and the same time limit. Those who do better in that prescribed time are treated as being successful. They are offered more avenues to grow and develop while others are marked as unsuccessful and left for lesser privileged opportunities in their career."

Maya said, "So true!"

I said, "Just like we think solving an issue faster is intelligence, we also think that making decisions in presence of more knowledge is intelligence.

Maya said, "I believe you don't agree with that too!"

I asked, "Of course there is no basis to such assumption. Do you agree that the knowledge is nothing but the memory?"

Maya said, "Yes. We discussed this last time. It is commonly understood that knowledge is an accumulation of information learned through different means. We also said that such idea of knowledge is illusory. But in all practical senses, we do treat memory of learned information as knowledge."

I asked, "Wouldn't you call the memory as a resource?"

Maya said, "If by resource you mean that it helps in serving a purpose, I would believe it is a resource."

I asked her, "Let us think of two scenarios. You give a similar task to two people. The task is to separate two metal pieces joined by four pairs of nuts and bolts. First person has a tool box with all kinds of tools. You can call the first person as having all the resources he needs to do this job. The second person has hardly any tools. However, he does seem to have some common utilities like a thread, a knife, a few nails and a piece of a rod. You can say that the second person does not have enough resources to do the job. As you would expect, the first person easily separates the two metal pieces with help of an appropriate spanner within a matter of minutes. The second person has to struggle and spend at least a few hours before finally coming up with a trick to get a grip on the nuts with his collection of random utility items." .

I then asked Maya, "Who do you think is an intelligent person out of the two?"

Maya said, "In this case, what the second person did is clearly a sign of intelligence. He hardly has any resource to do the job, yet he has used his brain to come up with innovative way to solve the problem."

I said, "Don't we see here that intelligence is about doing the best with what you have? It seems, the more resources you have, the less intelligence you need to do any job."

Maya said, "Very true. With right kind of spanner, anyone could do the job. The real intelligence was to come up with a solution despite lack of proper resources."

I said, "Can we say that our idea that more memory in terms of knowledge and learning indicates more intelligence might not be a realistic expectation? In fact, the intelligence seems to have no correlation to the amount of knowledge or experience.

Maya said, "That sure seems true, especially because knowledge or experience is nothing but the right resource for coping with different situations in our lives. At most, we could call those people to be conveniently equipped to solve most of the problems. But to call everybody with a lot of knowledge and experience as intelligent would not be a wise thing to do."

I said, "So, an idea of higher level of knowledge or intelligence based on memory, or speed is an illusion?"

Maya said, "I have no doubts."

Illusion of Human Only World

The universe contains billions of species, not just humans. Our understanding and treatment of the world from a human-only perspective is far from reality.

One evening, when I was browsing through some random posts on social-media, something suddenly caught my attention. There was a picture of water dripping from a hand-pump with a caption. Hand-pumps are quite common in rural areas which allow the underground to be raised by moving the handle. The caption said, 'Save Water! It is precious." Maya noticed that I was smiling so she wanted to have a peek too. When she saw the picture, she could not figure out what made me react to that picture.

She asked, "I don't understand it; what's so funny?"

I said, "This post wants to convey a message that water is precious and it should not be wasted. But I don't see any wastage in this particular situation."

Maya said, "I still don't understand. The picture is showing the water dripping from the handpump and is being wasted in the ground."

I asked her, "Where is the water coming from?"

She looked at the picture again and was quick enough to figure out the stupidity of the post. The water was being raised by the hand pump from the ground and any water not collected for a good use was going back to the ground. There was no water being wasted. On the contrary, it was going back to where it came from, to be pulled up again at a later time.

I said, "Though this is a particularly funny example of how we fail to see any situation in a broader perspective, we certainly live in a big illusion of what our world really is."

Maya asked, "And what is that?"

I said, "We have been conditioned by our habits, social practices, culture, religion, governance, education and language for thousands of years. We continue to live on this planet with a very limited understanding of our environment. We have made a very simplistic view of the world. Our vision of the world contains just three things: the earth, the humans and everything else seen either as a resource or a threat to humans. We spend all our life going after the resources for human consumption or trying to escape from the threats posed by different things we encounter."

Maya didn't say anything. She was trying to figure out if there was anything wrong with the way we live on this planet. Her mind started racing and different thoughts started coming to her mind. It was true. After all, we spend the whole life doing exactly this. We try to make use of the resources such as trees, minerals, water, fishes and different animals to make our life comfortable. While we do so, we also continue to save ourselves from the threats posed by dangerous plants, animals

126

insects, viruses or uncertain weather conditions such as storms, earthquakes or floods. It is always about us, the humans. Our idea of the world is really very simple; it contains humans and everything else either favorable or unfavorable for humans. Her train of though came to a halt as she saw me speaking.

I asked Maya, "What do you think we do when we see everything in terms of opportunities or threats?"

Maya said, "If something is a resource, we try to find ways to efficiently use them so that they serve larger number of people or last as long as possible."

I said, "True. And likewise, if something is a threat, we try to find ways to protect humans from them."

Maya said, "That is right. And we remove all obstructions which stop us or slow us down in getting the benefits from those resources."

I said, "This is why, we are never able to look at our universe with unconditioned point of view. We are obsessed with our species and its survival so much that everything happening around us is seen in terms of human issue. We come up with the illusory ideas of preservation or reduction of wastage of resources which leads us to worry about 'saving' the resources for future (human) generations."

Maya suddenly interrupted me by asking, "Wait! How is the idea of preservation or reduction of waste an illusion?"

I said, "You already know that our minds are always attached to the idea of permanency. We have already discussed that such an idea of permanency is an illusion because the reality is always changing. Nothing remains in the same state indefinitely and comes to face the unknown changes. With the illusion of permanent existence of things, we not only look at everything around us as resources specifically made for human consumption, but we are also continuously worried about their longevity. We worry about an insecure future when we won't have enough water to drink or sufficient fuel to generate energy."

Maya said, "I can understand what you are saying but can still not understand what's wrong with the way we have been living."

I said, "If you want me to say it simply, I would say that it is stupid of us to think that the world is only about us. The reality is that if every possible resource finished and every single human died on the planet, the universe will still continue to exist in form of millions of life forms. Even if you take this thought further and assume that all the water and oxygen got finished on the planet, then too will the universe continue to exist. The nature knows how to evolve, and in a matter of few million years, there might possibly be some life form that thrives on hydrogen, which might happen to be abundant at that time on this planet."

I continued, "But to come back to our point, we are the only species on our planet which has been given the gift of awareness. Only in this human form, we can understand how the world can be perceived differently by different life forms. We can imagine and appreciate how this world of an aquatic animal (as perceived by them) is different from the world of a bird. Instead, we choose to live a life of unawareness and see our universe as a human-only world, just like any other lower form of living creatures."

Maya said, "I am still not sure why talking about conservation or wastage is a bad idea."

I asked Maya, "Have you watched documentaries on wild lives predators hunting and killing their preys to satisfy their hunger and consuming them for their own survival?"

Maya said, "Yes, I have seen a lot of such programs."

I asked her, "What happens when the wild animals are done eating their prey?"

Maya said, "Once a lion or the wolves are finished eating their prey, the leftover is eaten by other animals."

I said, "That is true. Those who feed on the dead animals are called scavengers."

Maya said, "I know. We have also studied this in our schools. When the scavengers feed on the dead bodies, they convert the organic matter of those bodies back into the nutrients that get recycled into the eco-system."

I said, "You mean to say that whatever is left by the predators, is finished off by the scavengers."

Maya said, "Yes. And anything left might be consumed by other life forms such as rats, reptiles, and ants. Anything still left is decomposed by bacteria. Most of the organic matter will eventually be washed away into rivers, oceans or absorbed into the earth."

The recycling is not just limited to animal life, but to every little piece in this universe. The plants and trees too lose their leaves, fruits and flowers over their lifetime. The parts of trees which wither away due to changing weather, wind, sun or other natural causes, get decomposed and become part of the earth again. I knew that this fact was known to everybody. We all look at different activities going on around us but chose to ignore it because it does not seem to be relevant to our human world. If there is something that is inconvenient to us, we do not hesitate to destroy even if it amounts to wiping out the whole species. We do it to termites, rodents, poisonous insects and countless other life forms. There is no denying the fact that humans need to do what is necessary for their survival, but the way they do is out of an instinct of survival and not out of awareness, compassion or a superior intelligence that they must be capable of.

I said, "You are saying that there is no wastage in reality."

Maya was quiet. She knew what I was trying t o say for all this time. The universe was not just about humans and their opportunities in terms of resources. The universe was a continuously ticking interchange of various life forms undergoing a never-ending transformation. There was nobody either serving or being served. Nobody eating or being eaten. In fact, the whole chain of action of feeding is so inter-mixed that no one can be seen as the ultimate owner of the planet. The universe belonged to humans as much as it belonged to any other live or dead form existing for however small time. Yet, we have not only imagined it as a human universe, we have committed ourselves to take full control of every single activity that goes on around us.

Maya said, "I think I understood what you are trying to say. I can relate this to the common behavior we exhibit in our everyday lives. We look at different environmental phenomena from a human perspective. On one hand, when we encounter a forest fire, we see it as a huge destruction and a loss of precious resources, though it does not matter to us if it is the quickest way for the nature to refresh and renew itself to embrace the change in its landscape. On the other hand, when we notice that our continued use of toxic wastes, plastics and gases hurts other life forms on land and in oceans, we do not seem to care. We worry about the burning of forests because we lose our resources, but we do not care about damage to millions of other life forms because apparently, their lives (or death) does not affect us. They are not a part of human-universe to us."

I was quietly listening to her. There was something more to it. Our illusion or the universe was not just limited to seeing it from a human point of view. Even in this human universe, we live a life restricted by our own personal biases. We are severely limited in perceiving and responding to countless signals received from everything around us. As a result, what we see, hear or sense is an extremely simplified and incomplete view of the world. I was waiting for Maya to ask a right question before I could start exchanging my thoughts with her.

10

Our Personal Universe

All efforts to grasp, remember and communicate our existing world will invariably create and sustain the illusion because of our biases.

Maya told me, "Today I read something which doesn't seem to make sense."

I asked, "What was it?"

Maya said, "It said something like one must look at the world as it is, and not as one thinks it is."

I asked her, "What is your confusion?"

Maya said, "When I look at the world, I just look at the world. I don't know if there is any other way I could look at it. How could I know if I am not really looking at the world as it is?"

I said, "I can make it easy for you. We talked in the past about our illusion of separation. We exist in this world assuming ourselves to be detached from the world. For each of us this separation makes us view our world as having two distinct parts. Those two parts are me or mine and the others.

What we consider ours include our parents, our children, our relatives, friends, and the property we own. Anything that we do not relate to or we do not want to possess falls in the other category. In determining what is ours, the sense of ownership weighs much more than the sense of closeness."

Maya asked, "I don't understand the last part."

I said, "I said that being close to something or someone does not mean we might consider it our part. We consider something as ours only when we feel that we have full freedom to interact with it or control it. The physical closeness doesn't make something ours even if continues to be very near to us for many years."

Maya said, "That is true. There might be many things in and around our house such as various insects or birds which we don't find any closeness with."

I said, "You could imagine something even closer. One might have a mole on the face and might absolutely hate it being a part of one's body."

Maya said, "I understand it now. If something cannot be controlled by us, it cannot be ours. Everything that we like or like to have can be called as ours."

I said, "So, I was saying that one might live in a rental house for more than a decade and still not consider or treat it as one's own. On the contrary, a newly purchased house immediately becomes a very close part of us. On the same lines, one may stop considering one's children as one's own if they don't feel any sense of control over them. You might have seen many cases where parents send their kids out of their house, or even disown them. It is not just the physical objects, but even the ideas that we generate, we give them far more value than the ideas that belong to others. Our endless discussions and conflicts with each other's ideologies has its roots in the same philosophy. My idea is better than your idea. With such an idea of separation between ourselves and the others, when we view two objects, one of which happens to belong to us, our observation ceases to be a realistic view of the world. We instantly develop a bias splitting the world into two parts to create our unique version of the world around us."

Maya said, "If this is true, then I don't see any way we could get past this state. We all have some possessions, some friends and relatives who we feel close with. Does it mean that we all are bound to have a divided and biased view of the world we live in?

I said, "That is not true. All children are born with an unbiased point of view because they do not have any idea about what is theirs and what is not. The just go about anywhere, pick anything and talk to anyone with no reservation. They look at the world as it is; playful!"

Maya said, "It means that the world that adults see is not the world that the children see!"

I said, "True. The children have an unadulterated view of the world whereas the adults have a personalized version of their world with their own stock of likes, dislikes, jealousy, greed and desires of unlimited possessions."

Maya asked, "So, the world that we see is simply an illusion?"

I said, "An Illusion! Every person creates its own unique imagination to establish a world of bondage, conflicts and sufferings. No two people look at the world in the same way. You could say that each of us creates our own (copy of) world!"

Maya said, "I would like to know more about how viewing the world as a separation between mine and yours create a world of bondage, conflicts and sufferings."

I said, "When we look at the world with a divided perspective, we give different weightage to things based on who owns them. We give more value to things that we possess or the work that we do compared to others' possession or actions. We get a great satisfaction when we are working for ourselves or for the ones whom we consider ours. Psychologists call such a bias as Endowment bias where people tend to give more value to things just because they own them."

Maya said, "Yes. I know about this. In my elementary school, there was a girl in our class whose mom was our class-teacher. Everybody in our class knew the teacher was partial in treatment toward her daughter compared to other students."

I said, "This is a well-known human behavior. Our attachment to certain things or ideas or aversion to them affects our decision making. One of my friends was once summoned for a jury duty related to a case of car accident involving drunk driving. Before shortlisting the jury, the judge asked if any of us had religious or cultural reservations about alcohol use. My friend told her that his religion as well as his family values didn't look very highly of those who consumed alcohol. The judge then spared him from being a part of the jury because she was aware that his judgment about the case might not have been free of bias."

Maya said, "I can understand that whenever someone views the world, it is immediately divided into two parts, mine and not mine. With this illusory division, one views it with partiality giving the things one owns more weightage compared to the others. What if someone is in one's own home? I assume one owns everything in one's home. Would he or she view one's personal universe of one's own home in the way the things really are?

I was surprised by Maya's question. It was true. In the outside world, a person divides everything into mine and not mine. But in one's own home, one owns everything. She was questioning if at such times one can observe the world as it is. I was not sure. I never thought about it. It so happens that at many times children surprise us by coming up with the most brilliant questions.

I said, "I am surprised by your question! It seems like a favorable situation to check if one can view the world as it is in one's own home. Let's talk about it."

Maya said, "We all spend our time in this house. We own everything in this house. I would like to know if we are really seeing everything the way it is or not."

I said, "When it comes to buying something for the house, I and your mom have a different opinion. Whether we buy new washing machine, or we want to color our house, we have a hard time deciding about it. Even if we both come to agreement about paining the house, we are not able to agree on the right colors. At our own home, we all have our own opinions and we continue giving more weightage to our opinion. I am sure you must be having some doubts that we are treating you two sisters differently under some similar situations. Going past our personal relations, we can check if we are viewing different objects in the house free of any such conflicting bias. I don't like the toothpaste your mom uses, and she doesn't like the clothes I buy. She hates the way my clothes are lying around the house and I hate that she wakes up late in the morning."

Maya was laughing. She said, "Ok, I get it! No matter how personal our space is, we will not stop dividing the world between what we like and what we don't. Simply speaking, there is no way we can easily go past our ideas of mine and not mine."

Maya the asked me, "Don't we do the same with not only the things we own, but also with the things we create?

I said, "Yes. We assign more value to things we create and get great satisfaction from doing that. In fact, people love to buy furniture from the IKEA stores just for this very reason that they get to 'make' their own furniture. You would find it funny that this behavior is actually known as the IKEA effect."

Maya said, "I can see great dangers with this kind of bias."

I asked her, "What do you mean?"

Maya said, "The very idea that a thing or a process is better (than other) just because you made it, seems to lack the sincerity."

I sensed what she was going to say. Yet, I asked her, "why do you think it lacks sincerity?"

Maya said, "All is good if one is alone and doing something by himself or herself. If I bring a furniture from IKEA and feel great in making it myself, it does not affect anybody. But I am worried what happens when more people work together. Don't you see how it would be a problem when two or more people work as a team or a few hundred people work as a company or millions of people work as a country?"

I said, "You are trying to say that when people work together in a group, each one will give more weightage to his or her own contribution."

Maya said, "Yes. We imagine that when two people come to work together, they achieve more than the two could achieve individually. I have heard people quoting the statement about one and one making eleven. Don't you also say that when your company merges with another company then the two companies will achieve more than what any one could achieve because of the synergy from combined activities?"

I said, "Yes, that is true. We do have many instances where two entities working in harmony can achieve greater than what each individual can by working alone."

Maya said, "But that is only possible when the two work in harmony. From what you have explained about one's tendency to divide the world into two parts, mine and not mine, it is difficult to imagine two random people working in harmony. When each person will tend to give more weightage to one's own contribution in terms of opinions or efforts, how do you imagine a harmony?"

I said, "I think you made a valid observation. If two people work together, they both will see their own contributions to be important and worthy. When millions of them come together as a nation, the country will have its own bias towards its policies, its contributions to the world and its threats and opportunities. We all know that in many international disputes relating to business, national borders or foreign policies, none of the country thinks it's stakes are inferior to other countries."

Maya said, "If we all have an inherent bias of feeling more attached to our own property, ideas and efforts, we cannot work together in harmony. Is it not right?"

I said, "True! The idea of synergy or harmony seems like an imaginary expectation for most of us. Too bad, things don't seem to happen the way we expect."

Maya asked, "Is there not a way to be able to look at the world as it is without any bias? Can we not attain the state of harmony?"

I said, "I would want you to come up with an answer. You know the real reason behind why we cannot see the world as it is. It is because we see everything from the perspective of mine and not mine that we create a division in this world."

Maya said, "If the only reason for the division is the idea of me and you, or mine and not mine, then this division has to go for the harmony to exist."

I said, "That is right. Can you imagine what can make this division to go?"

Maya thought for some time. She could not figure out how the separation of me and not me from people's minds could be gone. She said, "I don't know. I don't think there is any way we could remove such tendencies from our minds."

I said, "It is actually very easy. Do you realize that the idea of me or you cannot exist alone in absence of other?"

Maya asked, "How come?"

I said, "Think a little. What happens when the idea of 'I' is gone? Is there any way 'You' can exist if the 'I' is gone?"

Maya thought for some time. She said, "Oh! I see it. No, if I don't exist, then there is no way you can exist either. It is like we don't bother about something when we are not involved in it. It is only when we have an interest in something, we start getting involved and soon create an idea of likes and dislikes about issues related to this. When we hear someone only talking about himself or herself, we don't care to listen. It is like, if I am not the part, then I don't care what you do. For a division to exist, both we must exist."

I asked, "So the way we can start working in harmony with each other or start seeing the world as it is when the idea of division between me and you is missing. And all we need is the idea of any one of us to go – either myself of you. Let us think of a situation where the idea of the other is missing?"

Maya tried to think but could not find any answer.

I said, "In love! There is no other in love. When the idea of the other person is gone, all that remains is one single communion."

Maya thought for some time. She didn't say anything. She knew that in love the distinction between mine and yours ends, because for the one in love, there is no idea of other. When there is no such division in love, there is no separation. She knew that idea of separation was an illusion. She had seen

141

mother birds making endless trips to feed their babies ignoring their own need to feed themselves. Most animals otherwise, get food for themselves. For a mother, the child is not another person. A child is a part of herself. It was so simple. It was Love that breaks the illusion. The illusion of separation, distinction and multiplicity.

Maya asked, "Is there any other way besides love where our illusory division ceases to exist so that we could view the world as it is without discrimination?"

I said, "The first way was to lose the sense of other person. This kind of behavior is seen in love. The other way to get rid of such distinction is to lose oneself. In any encounter of a fresh kind where no previous memory or experience can be imagined, the world is seen as it is. An idea of me or myself can only exist if previous association with the current experience can be remembered. In a fresh encounter, everything around you is new, and you don't see yourself related to it in any way."

Maya said, "When do we experience that?"

I said, "We do. When everything is new to you. For example, when you are in a foreign land about which you haven't known or heard much about. Once I had a chance to visit England for the first time. From the moment I entered the airport, I started seeing everything for the first time. I was noticing with great interest, the cleanliness of the place, the moving belts carrying the luggage and the courtesy of people handling different jobs. The ride in the aircraft was a new experience for me. I liked the seats, the services, the food and everything that happened in the flight. When we landed in the new country, I saw the clean roads, fast cars, beautiful buildings, complex network of trains and the variety of things to eat in the breakfast at the hotel. I liked the weather even though it was extremely cold. I liked to walk purposelessly for miles on the streets despite the chilling and rainy weather."

Maya said, "From what I understand, you were going through all the experiences without comparing or expecting. You were not comparing or expecting because you never knew anything like that in the past. With no knowledge of the past, there was no idea that belonged to you or your experiences in context of your experiences in the new place. There was no idea of 'I' which could give rise to expectations or comparisons."

I said, "That's right. This is what was happening with me. The place, its culture and environment were new, there was nothing which I could call as mine or not mine. 'I' and 'you' are the two opposite poles; in absence of one, the other cannot exist. In absence of any such discrimination, all I was observing was in its absolute form, as it was supposed to be.

Maya said, "What happens when we encounter those things again which you lived completely in your first experience without comparisons and expectations?"

I said, "When we continue to live through the similar experiences every day, we tend to start associating and dissociating with various things based on our liking. Soon we become habitual of the same breakfast, same routine and the same buildings. With the newness and freshness gone, we start losing our attention on the things that we observed with great interest in our initial encounter with them. With continued exposure to the same experiences, we become slaves of our likes and dislikes as the division between mine and not mine starts building slowly."

Maya was listening quietly. She said, "If I were to break the illusion of this division so that I could have a fresh encounter with the universe every day, I will have to simply love. I will have to keep looking at everything with fresh eyes every moment!"

I was glad that I was able to put this idea in a simple manner for her to understand. I thought of proceeding ahead to tell her about a few more ways we continue to discriminate between the things looking from a biased perspective. I said, "Our discriminatory lookout in viewing things based on our possession of them also creates a psychological conflict within ourselves. In a realistic world, one would imagine that the pain of losing an object would equate to the value associated with its acquisition. On the contrary, it is seen that once we acquire something, our pain of losing it becomes much more because of our disproportionate valuation of the things that we own. You can easily relate that the pain of losing a ten-dollar bill is far more than the pleasure of finding a ten-dollar bill on a street. This habit of loss aversion is one of the biases that translates the real world into the world of conflicts for us. We don't feel the pain of others in the same way as we feel our own pain. It would not come as a surprise that the ideas of pains and pleasures are born out of our own mind, due to the imperfect way we perceive the world around us."

Maya said, "I find it difficult to accept that people would not feel other's pain in the same way as they feel their own."

I said, "It is easy for you to say because you are still very young. It is not true that people do not understand pain or suffering of everybody at all times. However, it is also true that they are unable to look at all the situations without introducing a bias. People tend to pay more attention to immediate, relatable things in front of them. They generally tend to feel more sympathetic towards specific type of a victim in comparison to a large vaguely defined group with the similar needs. This behavior is known as the identified victim effect whereby people are more inclined to help identified individual victim compared to a group of people with the same need."

Maya said, "It's sad. I can't stop wondering how our minds looks at the world so differently because of its unique ways!"

I said, "There is also something good about knowing how the mind works with such a bias. It is only when you know how things work, you can work around their tendencies to achieve what you want. I see that every year in my office, the human resource department promotes a campaign for the benefit of a charitable trust. The company advertises such that more people can relate to their campaign and come forward to contribute. Their posters contain individual faces with name and a brief description. They are aware of the identified victim tendency in the minds of people and know how to tap it for the advantage of the larger community.

I continued talking about different psychological tendencies of human mind which created an illusory world for us. I said, "There is another known human behavior called effort justification, where people tend to show asymmetry in comparing two outcomes. They are commonly seen to attribute a higher value to the outcome of some task that they have put efforts into. You might have seen people cherishing their first earned salary or being attached to an ugly looking piece of part which they made themselves."

Maya smiled. She knew that it was a common behavior. She said, "Don't you love the tomatoes that grow in our little kitchen garden? I doubt if you would ever pick similar tomatoes from a grocery store. Since you have put efforts into growing them yourself, you don't look at them the same way as you would look at any others. To you, they are simply the best!"

I had to admit she got me there. I continued, "The illusory division of the world between oneself and the others seems to manifest in many more ways. When it comes to success, people can be seen to attribute their own skills, efforts and characteristics responsible for their success. This self-serving bias also makes them blame all of their failures to the forces outside their control."

Maya said surprisingly, "So, we behave differently for success and failures just like we treat a gain and a loss differently!"

I said, "Very true. It seems you are getting the pattern. It's always about oneself versus the others and it works in the same manner towards possession, opinion, effort, or relationships. People generally display illusory superiority in the sense that they overestimate their own qualities and abilities in relation to the same qualities and abilities of others."

Maya said, "So, looking at the same task, when they rate it for themselves, they think it is superior while other's is not so good?"

I said, "That's right. At other times, when observing others, people tend to make fundamental attribution error which is sometimes also known as correspondence bias. They

146

tend to believe that what people do reflects what they are. In other words, people's interpretation of their own behavior is different than their understanding of other's behavior. In explaining the behavior of other people, they tend to put undue emphasis on their internal characteristics rather than the external factors."

Maya said, "I don't understand what is meant by internal characteristics or external factors."

I said, "I can explain that. Consider a situation where you see a person driving very fast on a road. You would be inclined to assume that he is a rash driver, or that he is insensitive about others on the road. It would not occur easily to you that he might be actually in some emergency which might have forced him to forget about everything else in his surroundings."

Maya said, "I understand. If they happen to make mistake, they have many explanations related to external factors such as light not being sufficient, or the broken pencil, or the delayed train. But if someone else seems to be late or his work is not satisfactory, they will assume them to be lazy, insincere or irresponsible."

I said, "Very true! We do a poor job in understanding people in general. In estimating oneself or others, people are susceptible to do many mistakes. It so happens that people with lower skills usually overestimate their capabilities whereas highly skilled people tend to underestimate their capabilities."

Maya said, "I think I might have come across similar situations in our schools, but I always thought it was someone's peculiar behavioral trait."

I said, "No, it is not an isolated individual possibility. This kind of behavior is actually known as Dunning-Kruger effect."

I had given enough ways in which humans look at an unbroken reality and create a bias between what they think is theirs and that which they think is outside them. I said, "I think you might be getting an idea about the illusory picture we create out of the world which in reality might nowhere be close to our understanding of it. It so happens that we are never able to see things the way they are. It is not possible even if we try to make conscious attempts to get rid of any bias in ourselves.

Maya asked, "It seems we all do a pretty bad job of understanding people including ourselves. Is there any other reason why we fail to understand the reality the way it is?

I said, "There are many more ways in which we create a gap between the reality and our understanding of it. One way in which we come to know about the world is through communication. We spend lot of time sharing a lot of information verbally or through messaging. It is our selective attention to some parts of information that leads us to get an incomplete picture of reality."

Maya said, "That could be really bad. If a same piece of message is passed among many people such that each person passes a selective information to the next, the end message may be totally different than the original one."

I said, "That is what really happens in the world. We not only get pleasure in passing on different kinds of messages to people, we certainly believe most of such message that we receive to be true. This tends to create an illusory idea of the world we live in, a world in our mind based on the distorted information collected through different mediums."

Maya asked, "How does that happen?"

I said, "The reason behind such behavior is that when we hear someone speaking to us, our mind has to work with a lot of information in a very short amount of time. To grasp the fast inflow of information, it tends to capture the key words and ideas while ignoring most of the other information depending on when and how it was said or how important it felt. One such behavioral habit is known as Serial Position effect. When you hear a list of things, you tend to remember those which were said in the very beginning or at the very end. You would find it much harder to remember what was said in the middle."

Maya said, "It is interesting!"

I said, "I know. There is yet another theory which the psychologists call as Recency effect. They say that when you are asked to recall items in a list in any order, you would remember those at the end of the list more easily than others. There is another theory known as Primacy effect, according to which people can recall the items in the beginning of the list with greater ease than items in the middle.

Maya said, "From all this, it seems that people would not easily remember anything that was said in the middle of a long message. If someone were to influence others more easily, they would put the information they want to convey in the beginning and the end of their speech and everything else that they don't want them to pay attention in the middle."

I said, "That's so true."

I continued, "Besides how the message was conveyed, it also matters how important the information is to the listener. The mind tends to ignore all irrelevant information. This helps in remembering only the key information which a person thinks is valuable to him or her. It does not matter if the key information is a good one or a bad one. A person will always remember good or bad memorable events equally as long as they are relevant ones."

Maya said, "This means that not only will we tend to carry good and bad memory of key events, we will easily forget all that we didn't find worthy of noticing. In this way we continue to see what we want to see and hear what we want to hear. In other words, we care only for those things which we feel important. We cannot see the world as it is. We can only see it as we are."

I thought of stopping at this time. It was not that the whole list of human biases was exhausted. There were more than hundred more such human traits, talking about which would convey the same idea repeatedly. It was clear that humans would not be able to go past their biases to miss the reality of even the human universe in a big way.

It seems Maya had found the answer to her question. She wrote on the whiteboard.

> **We cannot see the world as it is. We can only see it as we are.**

Illusion of Birth & Death

*Every moment the reality changes appearing
to create and destroy different forms.*

Maya had been taking marching band classes in her school. One day she asked me to come and see their final performance. I went to the school which was holding the band competitions. There were more than fifty teams from different schools around the state. The whole program lasted a few hours. Her show was in the end, so she accompanied me in the first half, watching the performances of other schools. It was a magical experience watching a large group of students playing band while marching on the ground and making formations. Soon Maya left so that she could be with her team on time. In a couple of hours, all the schools were done with the show and we started back to our house. Maya seemed excited as her team had won the second position.

When we were driving back, I told Maya that I really liked their show, especially the formations that the students made while playing their instruments. Maya said, "We are just doing simple formations. Our main effort has been on the marching and the band music. But I can show you what some of the teams do in other places."

When we reached home, she ran and grabbed a computer to show me a video of a band performance. The clip showed a team playing a song of Michael Jackson while marching and making some formations. Soon the whole group of band players surprisingly moved and rearranged such that they looked like a giant human shape resembling Michael Jackson himself. The huge shape not only looked like him but was also maneuvering his signature moon walk. It was a unique experience watching a huge animated Michael Jackson move on the ground dancing and seemingly playing one of his famous songs. As soon as the performance ended, the band players dispersed and the huge animated dancing star got lost in the scattered band players.

Picture 9: Creation or destruction of a form out of the existing matter. It is both real as well as an illusion.

I said, "Wow! That helps understand the nature of illusion! There were just a group of band players moving on the ground and yet we saw a huge shape emerge among the band players to sing and dance for us!"

Maya said, "I knew you would like that. I too get excited about it every time I look at this performance."

I said, "You do know that big moving image we saw among those band players was just an illusion! There was nothing like him anywhere before they started playing the band or at the end except for the individual band players, and yet an image was born out of the same group of people to sing, dance and finally get lost among them."

Maya said, "Yes. I know. The image of the singer, its birth, its dance and its dissolving into the band was just an illusion."

I asked her, "I am sure you know why you call it an illusion."

Maya said, "Of course. We had talked about the rules of illusion some time back. We said that imagining a form is an illusion when there is none. We also said that creating a reality is an illusion when there is none. Here we not only imagined a form that looked like Michael Jackson, but we also experienced his dance moves. In reality, it was an imagined form made up of many band players moving around and rearranging themselves."

I asked her, "So you are convinced that nothing really was born when a large group of band players assembled such that a form was imagined. Likewise, you also agree that nobody had vanished when at the end of their performance, all the band players dispersed, and the big dancing form simply collapsed."

Maya said, "Sure. There was nobody dancing there. The form was created out of the assembly of the band players which got destroyed when they disassembled at the end of their performance."

I asked Maya, "So you are convinced that a birth and a death are simply illusions?"

Maya was surprised, "What! When did I say that? I simply agreed that the birth and the death of the image of Michael Jackson in this video of marching band was an illusion."

I asked, "Is this not obvious, though?"

Maya said, "I don't know how is this obvious. A birth is something real. We can see something new coming into existence, something that was never there in the first place. A death is real too. Someone who dies is lost forever. We see it happening all the time. You can't call them illusions."

I said, "Let's see closely at what his happening at the band performance in the video. At the beginning and at the end, we see a group of band players performing on the ground. However, at all other time, we failed to notice the band players individually or as a group. We only noticed a big human form moving and dancing in front of us. What do you think made us see a human form even when the band players never left their place from the grounds?"

Maya said, "We were able to see the marchers in the beginning and the end because they were not forming any special shape that could steal our attention. They were randomly moving around."

I asked, "Does it mean that it was the rhythmic and synchronized arrangement of those band players that made us forget their individuality and focus on the whole structure as one big form?"

Maya said, "That looks like what has happened here. The band players were always there. It was the synchronization between them that made us forget their individuality and look at them as one big combined form."

I said, "So, as long as all the team players were moving and interacting together in harmony, our attention was lost from their individuality and moved on to the new form that emerged from this perfect interaction among themselves.

Maya said, "I can see that the harmony and close interaction of all the band players made us experience the presence of a new form. I still do not understand why you said that a birth or a death is an illusion.

I said, "Everything in nature is happening exactly as we just saw in this video. That we see as a birth of a new form is not any creation out of nothingness. It is simply a coming together of different elements to establish a harmonious interaction. As long as the close interaction and synchronization of those elements continues, the form seems to be alive. That we realize as a newly created form is still the combination of all those elements, but we do not notice them as they are individually or as a group. All we notice is the new form created out of those elements working in a harmony among each other. Since everything in nature continues to change, such synchronization or harmony between any group of elements cannot continue to exist forever. Eventually the end of such interactions between different elements makes us lose our focus from the (imagined) form back to the individual elements.

I said, "In a way, you could say that a birth (for us) is the coming into existence of something in our awareness. Similarly, a death (for us) is the cessation of existence of an idea or a thing in our awareness. Simply speaking the birth and death is from our own perspective, from the point of view as observers!"

Maya said, "You said that the birth and death happens in our mind. How do you explain the real experience of them happening every moment in this universe?

I said, "The birth and death as an idea of creation and destruction of 'something' are illusions. The idea of that 'something' which holds a real existence is a myth. We already talked about that core content of any object which is the central idea of its *Self*. It is that *Self* which is known as taking birth when a solidified idea of a thing comes to one's awareness for the first time.

Maya said, "I don't understand. Can you please explain with some example?"

I said, "You take some clay and add water to it. Slowly you start giving it some shape. For a while, the thing in your hands simply looks like an irregular shaped lump, and you don't associate the shape with anything you understand from your memory. You work on the lump of clay for some time, trying to give it some form. Eventually, a moment comes when you recognize the shape in your hands and call it a vase. At that moment, when you become aware of it as a shape, you experience the birth of a vase (from the clay). You could similarly describe it as the death of the vase too when I crush the newly formed shape back into a lump of clay."

156

Maya said, "You mean to say that all the time there was only the lump of clay in my hands. Yet, I experienced a birth and subsequently a death of something called a vase during this time. The vase was simply an idea in my mind, which was already existing in my mind before I experienced its birth. Just like the Michael Jackson being born and destroyed among a large group of band players moving in harmony on the ground. In fact, the form of Michael Jackson was never a different and a separate reality from the performing band players. Yet it seemed to have its own separate individuality."

I said, "You just said a very intelligent thing. There were marching band people as well as an image of a dancing superstar on the ground. Even though these two are totally distinct perceptions, they are not detached from each other. You can never separate one from the other, yet they both exist distinctly perceptible to us. Just like a clay is not different than the pot, the image of the star is not detached from the band players. The idea of separation between the two is an illusion."

Maya said, "If that is the case, then an individual cannot be isolated or detached from the society which is nothing but a collection of individuals in large numbers."

I said, "That is very true. Do you know what it means?"

Maya said, "It means that since there is no real separation between an individual and a society, there is no way one thought which prefers social rights above individual rights can be better than the other thought which prefers individuals above society. If seen carefully, a society is nothing but the individuals and an individual is just the reflection of the society.

I said, "So true! Coming back to the idea of birth and death, what is born and what dies is simply an idea. We tend to take the birth and death as real because our minds get attached (or repulsed) with the newly born things which could be an object, person or an idea. Once something gets attached with the mind either as a likeable thing or as a hateful thing, its existence is felt real. It is easy to imagine the existence of something as real, if that something can lead to real emotions of happiness or sorrow."

Maya asked, "So what exactly is a birth or a death?"

I said, "We already talked about objects. We said that there is no such thing as an object, there are only the assemblies of more objects. A birth of an object can be understood as a coming together of many separate smaller objects or assemblies to give an impression of one bigger object. Conversely, a death is the separation of a so-called object which is nothing but an assembly of different smaller objects, into two or more different such assemblies of objects through dispersal or destruction."

To illustrate this fact, I showed her two pictures. On the left there were few pebbles. On the right there were the same pebbles but moved and arranged in a specific manner. Seeing the two pictures as a sequence in time, the coming together of those pebbles could be seen as a birth of a square. Nothing had changed. There were same number of pebbles in the two situations. Yet, in the beginning there were only pebbles and no trace of anything like a square. Later, a square was noticed. One could call it a birth of a square which could be depicted as an emergence of a new creation which wasn't there in the beginning except for its idea.

Picture 10: A birth is an illusion of a preconceived form created out of rearrangement of elements

Maya was quietly observing the birth of the square among the pebbles. There were pebbles all along. But the square was something new that was being created. Created out of nowhere. She asked, "So, can we understand a birth as an integration of different things to give an impression of a new form? In the same way, could we say that a death is a disintegration of such a form?"

I said, "True. Integration and disintegration are a better word in place of birth and death. In fact, saying it like that makes one rooted in reality, and not be deluded with the painful illusion arising from the idea of birth and death."

Maya was surprised. She asked, "Why do you call the illusion of birth and death as painful?"

I tried to explain to her in simple words. "When something comes in the field of awareness, it's presence is noticed as a birth of a new entity. When the newly born form catches one's interest, it creates a sense of attachment. Once attached to a thing, person or a form, a person finds it painful to see this new possession to be destroyed or be lost. Losing an entity from one's perception or possession is nothing but its death.

Had there been no birth in the first place, the further attachment, pain and suffering would not be experienced."

I had tried my best to make her see this most complex mechanism in the fewest words. A birth or a death was a play of the mind. First, there was no real 'thing' to be born or to die. Second, there was no reality of birth or death. This all was a play of the mind. A birth was a creation of an idea of a personality (of an object or a person) in the mind of an observer. Similarly, a death was a cessation of the idea of the personality from the mind of the observer.

Maya asked, "So what if birth and death are illusions? Why should we even discuss whether they are real or imaginary? Can we not continue living our usual life treating them to be as real as we feel them to be?"

I said, "The birth of an idea or a form is the beginning of an entanglement. Once something has taken its place in your awareness, it can either make you attracted and attached to it or make you repulsed by it. The world of pleasure and pain exists in relation to things already known by you as real. A true knowledge of such illusions keeps you free from further attachments. Being free from attachment is to be free of pleasures and pains. When you notice a mirage in the desert, you know that the wet surface in your vision is an illusion. You don't get upset when you go near and find that it has vanished. In the same way, you don't get sad when the image of the Michael Jackson vanishes at the end of the band show. You only get hurt about someone dying or leaving you when you imagine them to be real and have attachment with them."

160

Maya asked, "If birth and death are simply illusions and if knowing them as illusion can help someone get rid of pains of attachments, then what is the way to get out of this illusion?"

I said, "A birth or a death happens when one is not aware. Look at the example of the pebbles. If you do not lose your attention, you can see the whole activity of the mind clearly. You can see the mind observing the emergence of a pattern from the randomly scattered pebbles, recognizing the pattern from its memory and associating it with a square shape. When you are so aware, you have already transcended from the illusion of birth and death (in this example). To be completely aware at the moments of birth frees oneself from the further attachments, suffering and pains resulting from such attachments. When one is aware of the possible birth of an entity, one can see it nothing more than the change of form in the field of reality. Such newly formed shape or an entity would still be known and identified as an object but will not result in the intense attachment that could cause suffering. In the event of the death of such an entity, an aware person would view this as a process of disintegration of the self, which was created at the time of birth. The person would know that such a self or an identity never existed before its birth. The person would have understood the reality of the birth, existence and the death of such a form as nothing but a transformation observed in the field of reality."

I was sure I had planted an idea about the illusory nature of birth and death in Maya's mind. It was only a matter of time, when she would be able to see the whole illusion with complete clarity. To know about an illusion paves way for its destruction.

161

12

Illusion of Duality & Opposites

*Our world of sorrows, sufferings or pleasure
is created due to our love for imagined
duality.*

I asked Maya, "If you ask a fish what it means to be wet, what do you think it would say?"

Maya was quiet. She didn't know what to say.

After some time, she spoke, "I don't think it would understand the question."

I asked, "Why? Is a fish not in the water all the time? Who else can tell us better than a fish what water is, or how it feels to be wet all the time?"

Maya said, "It is true that a fish is in the water all the time. Yet, I don't think it can know anything about wetness."

I said, "You are right about it. There is no way a fish can know anything about the water or about being wet. Have you wondered why it would be so?

Maya said, "I think I might know it somehow, but I cannot explain it."

I said, "That's ok. I can help you with that. I hope you know what it means not to be wet."

Maya said, "Yes. You are dry when you are not wet."

I asked her, "Will you understand what it means to be wet if you somehow know what it means to be dry?"

Maya said, "Yes. When I know what it is like being dry, I can see what it means to be wet."

I asked her, "Don't you mean to say that you can understand about wetness, when you have understood its opposite, the dryness?"

Maya agreed. She said, "Yes, the wet and dry are exact opposites. I can understand one in terms of another, but not any one of them individually without an idea of the other."

I said, "Don't you think that is the reason a fish can never understand wetness? It can live in water for its entire life being completely wet, but it has no means of understanding it because it has no way of knowing its opposite. For a fish, dryness is a non-existent feeling. A dry fish is a dead fish."

Maya said, "This is strange! Just because it cannot know dryness, it can never experience wetness even if it is entirely in contact with it!"

I said, "This is true with everything that can be known or experienced by us in terms of opposites."

Maya was excited, "I would love to know more. I don't think I ever got to hear something like this!"

I said, "The best idea to explore will be to take more examples of things which we know as pairs of opposites."

Maya said, "Let me think. What about freedom?"

I said, "Let's talk about freedom. What is freedom? How do you explain someone what is freedom? Can you tell me who desires freedom? Or who values freedom?"

Maya said, "From what you said earlier, it will not be possible for anyone to know the

> **"There is no concept of freedom to a person who is totally free".**

meaning of freedom if one has no idea of its opposite. The opposite of freedom is captivity, or bondage."

I said, "That is correct. It is true that there is no concept of freedom to a person who is totally free. Such a person who has never seen any captivity, bondage or restriction, it won't be easy for him or her to know about freedom."

Maya said, "I can see how simple yet so ridiculous it is. It is strange to imagine that the person who is totally free has no idea, concept, knowledge or even experience of freedom. To know what freedom is, one should first know its opposite. One has to lose one's freedom to know it, because only when something is lost, its opposite comes into existence."

I said, "Mankind has since hundreds of centuries longed for ultimate freedom. They imagine a kind of freedom where one has no idea of sorrow, pain or suffering. They imagine various kinds of gods, heavenly creations and paradises with never ending pleasures. They are unaware of the fact, that as soon as they imagine a concept of freedom, its opposite is born

165

at the same time. An idea of freedom cannot exist without an idea of captivity or bondage."

Maya said, "If to imagine or talk about freedom is not freedom, because it's opposite also exists at the same time, then what is freedom?"

I said, "Is it not obvious? The freedom that the fish has from wetness! It is in water all the time, yet it is unaware of its presence. For a person, who has no idea of either freedom or bondage, there is no knowledge of freedom. Such a state where someone is not even aware of freedom, is a freedom. A Freedom is devoid of the knowledge or concept of opposites, whether freedom or captivity."

Maya said, "It reminds me of something. I am sure you must have also read about this. I had never understood its meaning before this moment. Now everything has become so clear to me. It is a piece of writing about Freedom by Khalil Gibran from his collection called 'The Prophet'. He wrote,

"And my heart bled within me; for you can only be free when even the desire of seeking freedom becomes a harness to you, and when you cease to speak of freedom as a goal and a fulfilment."

It brought a smile on my face. "When even the desire of seeking freedom becomes a harness to you," I repeated.

I heard Maya saying, "I now remember I have always known this particular behavior in our everyday lives. Those kids who have never known poverty in their lives have no idea of luxury. They have seen, known and lived luxurious lives since the day they were born, yet they never seem to have any knowledge or experience of luxury. For them the air-

166

conditioned houses and cars are a natural feeling, and so are the comfortable beds and rich food. Their parents might have seen poverty or hardships in their lives, and by providing all sorts of comforts to their child, they imagine that they are providing a life of comfort and luxury to their child. It is an ignorance to believe that someone can acknowledge any experience without having seen the opposites. The only way the child can experience the rich life he is living is to get away from it and experience the poverty, hunger and hardship. Once the opposite of luxury is known and experienced, the value or experience of the rich life will be known."

I was happy to see her getting a feel of the duality. I said, "Let's take another example. It is about health. What do you think someone who has never been sick, say about being healthy?"

Maya said, "I think I can be sure about that. The person would not know anything about enjoying good health as long as the opposite has not been personally experienced."

I said, "How True! Would a person who has never had an attack of Asthma, know how it feels to be breathing fresh air effortlessly? Can we make small children understand what it means to get tired while they are running around or climbing stairs many times a day? It is only when someone has known the suffocation of an Asthma attack, he or she can appreciate the healthier state of breathing freely at other times. It is only after someone has noticed the increase sugar or cholesterol levels in his blood, that he or she can know the dangers of eating unhealthy. At all other times, such people do claim to know, but they haven't really experienced the true state of such knowing."

I continued, "In absence of the knowledge of the opposite, one is free of knowing. The only knowledge in such cases is the non-dual experience which cannot be understood or explained. A happy person will not be able to know anything about happiness. He will simply be happy. Such happiness will be free from duality as there is no alternative state to it. It is only when such a person experiences suffering, that it will start knowing the good times in future. It is at those times, one will know the happiness because one has now known what it means not to be happy. Such a person would have created an illusory world of duality, of two different states of happiness and sorrows. This is the illusion of duality, which creates our world into two distinct parts, good and bad, right and wrong, heaven and hell."

Maya said, "From what you said, no one really knows anything unless it's opposite has been known too."

I said, "Yes. Clearly, we have two kinds of knowledge. In absence of duality, we are free of knowledge and experience. We are very much a part of the universe, though we cannot understand or explain anything. However, in duality, we start experiencing the universe as if it is split into two contrasting halves. This makes us know and experience the universe through pleasure and suffering. That is nothing but an illusion. A Grand Illusion, caused by our association with the dual nature of our minds."

Maya said, "I didn't understand what you said about creating a whole illusory universe out of duality. Can you please make it simpler?"

I said, "You agree that the reality is what it is at every moment; devoid of any special meaning?"

168

Maya said, "I think I can agree to it."

I said, "What do we do when we try to grasp it, interpret it or describe it?

Maya said, "I am not sure."

I said, "Don't we introduce words to grasp, understand, describe or communicate?"

Maya said, "Yes, we do."

I said, "What happens when we try to describe a universe using words which have opposites?

Maya said, "Oh! I get it. When someone tries to describe or grasp some description which contains words of duality, one can easily understand."

I said, "What happens when someone doesn't describe or grasps description with words which have opposites?"

Maya said, "In that case there is really no meaning, no understanding. But I don't get it! If all we care about understanding through language, shouldn't we obviously use words of duality?"

I said, "The issue with words of duality is that they have knowledge of the both. One cannot exist without the other. In fact, one is the mirror image of the other. If you talk about goodness, then you have already introduced an idea about an opposite of goodness, something bad."

Maya said, "I don't understand how the idea of goodness contains the idea about badness too."

I said, "If I were to tell you that you should be good, what thoughts come to your mind?"

Maya said, "When I am told to be good, I start thinking of avoiding anything that is considered bad."

I said, "There you go! You have to know everything about bad things even if you want to be good, otherwise you won't know what to avoid."

Maya said, "What is the problem in trying to avoid things which are not considered good?"

I said, "We won't go into the discussions of right and wrong. Any such idea which has opposites is an illusory creation of our minds. We are saying that the world is out there at all the times in its fullness. In such fullness, we all exist in this universe in harmony with everything around us. The moment we try to grasp the reality and try to describe it, we create an artificial division in this otherwise singular universe by ideas of opposing nature. There was neither good nor bad, or right or wrong before we thought of introducing a meaning to it. The problem with opposing ideas is that they both exist together as a reflection of each other. One cannot exist singly without other. Can you imagine a coin with just one side, either heads or tails? Such an idea has no reality. When asked to do good, you were already aware of things that are not good. With ideas of good and bad, or right or wrong, we observe everything in this universe with an illusory idea of dual nature of this universe. Our belief that good can exist on its own without bad is our illusion."

Maya asked, "Why do you say that our belief that good can exist on its own without bad is our illusion?"

I said, "Have you noticed people's reaction when someone posts news, blogs or videos of some girl beating a boy publicly?"

Maya said, "Yes. Almost everybody praises the girl for her boldness and taking a stand for herself."

I asked, "How do you think you would react to this?"

Our belief that good can exist on its own without bad is an illusion.

Maya said, "I don't think that I would be in a situation to comment on something about which I haven't got much information. I can't simply assume that if a girl is abusing a boy, then it must be the boy's fault."

I said, "Why do you think people praise the girl for doing something which might be wrong under ordinary circumstances for a boy doing the same?"

Maya said, "It has always been the case that the boys are the ones to be abusive towards girls. Most of the people consider it wrong. They always wish for something that could stop the physical supremacy of males over the females."

I continued what she started, "As a result, when they see a female taking a lead and hurting a male, they are happy! The only way that can reverse a situation is by going to its exact opposite. People cannot imagine any other scenario. For them if one thing is bad, then its opposite must be good. The idea that there is no case of supremacy, either for males or females, is non-existent in peoples' minds. It is because the idea of supremacy is a relative one. The opposite of this has to be a relative one too. If male supremacy is bad, then the only thing one imagines is that female supremacy must be good."

Maya said, "Oh! I can see now. We are saying that everything that has an opposite is always available to us as pair. There is no way we can choose one and ignore other. If there are coins, there will be heads as well as tails. The idea of holding on to only good is our illusion. It can never be done without also holding on to the idea of bad, even if it might be buried deep in our subconscious."

I said, "That is right. So, where does this illusory idea of an ideal world based on dual nature take us? It makes us believe and do all sorts of stupid and dumb actions. Pick any self-help book or listen to any motivational speaker, and you will hear them preaching about practicing positive thinking. How would someone know what it means to think positive without knowing negativity? What would such a person do who has been conditioned to always think positive? Will such a person not carry a conflicted mind everywhere trying to hold on to anything which it considers as positive while discarding which it thinks is negative? A mind which was originally completely free of idea of positivity or negativity in absence of such immature teaching has now been turned into a discriminatory machine. Such a mind knows nothing except dividing the world of infinite possibilities into positives and negatives."

Maya said, "What else could we do if not teach people to be good?"

I said, "You don't teach a dog to be a good dog. Neither do you teach a bird to be a good bird. Why do you think humans need to be 'taught' to be good? Why is it hard to understand that a person could be good even without having

172

an idea of goodness? Is this not what we started our discussion with today? Like a fish who doesn't know what wetness is, a good person is one who doesn't know what goodness is. He is simply good. Would you find a humble person who knows that he is humble? On the contrary, anyone who knows about his or her humility is not humble anymore. All those who continue to practice forgiveness, humility or positivity are never going to achieve any of those qualities for this simple reason."

Maya said, "That makes sense. So, what you are saying is that one need not name, label or describe the reality, especially those which have opposites. The moment such words come into existence, the reality is turned into an illusory division of two contrasting halves such as black and white, or good and bad. I think I can carry this new learning into almost any other ideas that we encounter on daily basis. We are told that we should practice non-violence. It is similar to the idea of dryness for a fish. How would I ever know what is being asked of me unless I have understood the idea of violence? It is like expecting a lion to know that it is promoting violence by killing animals for its food. It won't do any good to ask the lion to embrace non-violence. It will be as useless as talking to a drunk person about dropping the habit of drinking. A drunk man has no concept of sobriety or a non-drunk state. I can clearly see the whole trap of duality now. Our dualistic approach of looking at this universe has created a totally different world, a world of opposites!"

I said, "Yes. As long as the mind is devoid of ideas, concepts, and descriptions, the reality is already present in its unadulterated form. In such a state, a human is enjoying its existence no different than any other creature in the world."

Maya had understood. The Reality exists without need of words and descriptions. The words are separative, and they come with pairs of opposites which divides the world apart into two distinct parts. The world continues to exist in the same way with or without the words and descriptions. However, the human interaction with language, descriptions and concepts turns the non-dual reality into a duality, an illusory world of *Maya*, the Grand Illusion!

13

Illusion of Time & Space

Our minds are always stuck up in the past
or the future, even though there has never
been any other time than the present.

It was Sunday afternoon and I had hardly returned from a trip to nearby grocery store when I saw Maya in the Kitchen. She was impatiently moving around near the cooking range. There was a pressure cooker hissing quietly on top of one of the burners. I asked her where her mom was and why she had a grumpy look on her face. She said that her mom had gone to bathroom and had asked her to watch over the pressure cooker. She was expected to turn the stove off and remove the cooker from the stove as soon as it whistled twice. I immediately knew the seriousness of the two-whistle cook time of the pressure cooker, because I knew my wife was very particular about how much the rice needed to be cooked.

"It seems like I have been standing here forever; this pressure cooker has no intention to make a sound!" She said with a frustration.

"A watched pot never boils! Don't you know that?" I said sarcastically.

Maya said, "What! I have never heard this. What does it mean?"

I said, "It means exactly what you are experiencing right now. Since you are watching over something in an anticipation of a result, it seems to take ridiculously long time."

Maya said sadly, "I know!" Suddenly the pressure cooker made a shrieking sound. Maya quickly turned off the stove and removed the cooker.

"This is strange! I was standing here for so long and it seemed as if nothing was happening with the cooker. And as soon as I have taken my eyes off, it is already done!" She said with an amazement.

I said jokingly, "We might even add to this proverb, that an unwatched pot boils immediately."

Maya smiled. She said, "I know this happens many times. The time seems to drag slowly when you are waiting for something to happen. And on the contrary, it seems to go faster when you are having a good time."

I said, "I agree. We have a very slow elevator in our office. Though there are only three floors in the building, it takes forever to move from the first floor to the third floor. You can imagine the frustration of being locked inside a small box and have nothing to do except staring at the floor indicator for what feels like an eternity."

Maya said, "I can relate the feeling as I have just experienced a similar one a few moments ago. I am sure, if the elevator was transparent and you could watch outside while it was moving, you wouldn't have realized that the elevator was

176

taking a long time. Your attention would have drifted away from the elevator's slow speed to something interesting outside."

I said, "That is true. The time interval seems big only when we are expecting some outcome. If we get distracted in other activity, the perception of the time changes and its slowness is not felt. It is not the actual time which expands or shrinks, but our perception of the time. This is why you can call the time as an illusion, which changes based on individual situation. In fact, the idea of both the time and the space are illusions."

Maya said, "Time and Space? I have never understood the meaning of these words. I have read that Einstein had developed some special theory of relativity based on time and space. But I won't dare to even think about such complex issue."

I asked, "What if I make it very easy for you to understand in what way time and space are comparable things and have illusory nature. It might be great if we were able to figure out the reason why they both seem to behave in such strange manner."

Maya said, "If understanding space and time would be easy, then I hope anything in this world would be easy. I can try to participate in the discussion with you!"

I said, "Let's start with what we mean by space and time."

Maya said, "Is space the separation between two objects?"

I said, "That seems like a good description. We will accept that to start with. Two objects are seen as two objects because there is a space between them; a separation. If we were to remove the space between them, we might not identify them as two separate objects."

I then asked Maya, "And what do you think time is?"

Maya said, "I know we use this word all the time but I am not sure how to describe it. I mean, I know that we measure time in seconds, minutes, hours, days, weeks, months and years."

I said, "Can we not say that time separates two events in the same way as the space separates two objects?"

Maya said, "Oh! Yes. It does make sense. The measurement of time in seconds, hours or months is nothing but the magnitude of the separation between two events."

I said, "So one thing is clear. We do understand that space and time seem to behave in the same way. They separate the things which we can perceive either through our senses or through our mind. In as much as we perceive physical objects through our senses of smell, touch, taste, vision and hearing, we perceive the time as a separation between two events registered in our memory. As we said, if the separation is missing then the two objects cannot be identified as two objects. This is true for space as well as time."

Maya said, "This is quite simple! A time or space is all about separation between two things."

I said, "Not only that. This separation between objects or events which we know as space and time is nothing but an illusion!"

Maya said, "I don't believe that!"

178

I said, "You will yourself see it once we talk about if further." Then I asked her, "What do you think the separation between two things signify?"

Maya said, "When the separation between two things is not much, we say they are nearer to each other. When there is a big separation, we say they are far from each other."

I asked her to confirm, "Do you mean to say that the idea of separation is reflected in terms of far and near or big and small between two things (in space) or events (in time)?"

Maya said, "I think so."

I said, "You are right. When the separation in space or time is noticed between the two things, it is experienced in terms of the magnitude of the separation. We notice this separation in terms of how far or near two things are. We may also seem to convey how big or small the impact of the things is on each other, based on their distance from each other. Whatever we may experience in such situation, one thing is sure that this all is nothing but an illusion of the mind."

Maya asked, "Which of these is an illusion - the idea of the distance itself, or the idea of the measurement of the distance?"

I said, "Both are illusory. First, the idea of the distance is an illusion. Which means that in reality two things which look separate might not be separate at all. Secondly, the idea about the distance of separation is an illusion too. Something that seems very far might not actually be as far. Or something that seems to be so big might not be actually so big."

Maya said, "I don't understand. You make some radically strange statements. If two things can be seen as separate, what is the basis to the conclusion that they might not be separate. Can we not notice and measure the distances or time intervals? If two things are one meter apart, then they are one meter apart, neither more nor less. In the same way if two events are two minutes apart, then there could not be a doubt whether it is more than one minute or less than an hour? Where is the case for any illusion here?"

I said, "You are right that in physical sense, you can measure the distance or time gap between two things or events. You are also right to say that there should not be a confusion in what is big or small, or what is far or near. A two-meter-long rod will always be longer than a one-meter-long rod. The measurement itself should be able to convey this information without any conflict."

Maya asked, "So, where is the catch?"

I said, "The catch is in the way such measurements are interpreted by the mind. What seems to be far away might not be felt as far. What seems to be right here, might really be felt as a faraway thing or an event. How we perceive any measurement in space or time has nothing to do with their actual physical presence. It is dependent on the relation between the two objects or entities, the perceiving and the perceived."

Maya asked, "Relation between the two objects? I don't understand."

I said, "The idea of separation is in mind. For a mother, her son might be thousands of miles away, but a single phone call about his accident may make her fill with grief. The physical distance between them is an illusion. In reality, there is no distance between a mother and her child."

Maya said, "I see! You are talking on a totally different level. All I was able to think was in terms of physical universe as it seems to exist and abide by the general laws of science. You are trying to look at the world from the level of the mind."

I said, "What is this world if not a play of the mind? Have we not already figured it out that there is no basis to the physical existence of the objective world? When investigated thoroughly, we found that there is no essence to anything physical in this world. When trying to find out the root cause of any action or movement, we saw that there is no single independent 'actor' ever responsible for anything that happens in this universe."

Maya said, "I remember. We had already talked about it. It is that this all is so radically different than my current perception of the kind of universe we think it is. It will be a while before I am ready to look at this world with a condition-free observation."

I smiled. It was true. Our minds have been conditioned by millions of years of human experience with this universe. We have been taking this illusory world as the real world for as long as we have lived on this planet. Old habits die hard. Investigation into the nature of our perceptions and a thorough understanding of all the illusions is not enough for the illusions to go away. It will require an unconditioned observation into the nature of things along with an unwavering attention to break away from the illusion, the *Maya*.

181

My thoughts were suddenly interrupted by Maya's voice asking, "You said that there is no separation between a mother and her child. I imagine that it is because of the mother's love for her child. Can I expect its reverse to be true too? Would someone we hate be very far from us?"

I said, "Yes. If love seems to close the gap between the two, the hate seems to carry an impression of a huge separation between the two."

Maya said, "I think this kind of behavior looks familiar. If I hate or dislike someone, I don't think I pay any serious attention to their presence or anything that relates to them. If such people are talking, I wouldn't be paying attention even though I might be hearing them speaking. It is like they were far away from me."

I said, "The idea of distance from someone is dependent on how you relate to them. If you love the other person or the thing, then its closeness to you does not depend on its physical separation. On the similar lines, if you don't like someone or something, its physical closeness will not make you feel closer. You would have noticed this yourself. When you are on your mobile phone or a computer chatting with your cousins, does it matter if they are physically separated from you by more than six thousand miles?"

Maya said, "True. When I am busy talking or texting with them, I forget that they are far away. For me their voices in my ears and my interaction with them does not let me be aware of the separation."

I said, "It is because there is really no separation at that moment!"

Then I asked her, "And what do you say about Christina, your neighbor?"

Maya said, "I see her every day at the bus stand. We sit together in the class too. But we haven't talked or looked at each other since our fight two months ago."

I said, "So, you are not so much separated by your cousins who are thousands of miles away but have a huge wall of separation between your next-door neighbor!"

I then asked her, "Can you see the kind of fabric that this whole space-time thing is made of?"

Maya asked, "Is it those whom we like, we find closer and those whom we don't like, we feel far away?"

I said, "The idea of separation seems to be related to our experience of pleasure and pain. It can be easily seen that the pleasure brings things closer to us and the pain sends the things or people away. This relation seems to be in direct proportion to the intensity of our experience. The more you like someone, the more you feel them closer to you. Likewise, the more you dislike someone, the farther you feel yourself from such person. Like your friend Christina, this person might be occupying the seat next to you, buy you would hardly register anything that this person says or do. The physical separation would mean nothing."

Maya said, "So it means that the separation between two things in space or time as measured by the instruments does not represent the measurement as picked by our senses."

I said, "Yes. A one hour spent by someone with his loved-one will pass very quickly whereas a one-hour class of

183

mathematics studying advanced algebra will feel like never ending, especially if one hate mathematics. A one-hour duration is not a fixed time interval to your senses of perception. It depends on the nature of relation between the two."

Maya asked, "So, can we say that our perception of space and time as the idea of separation between two things, people or events is not fixed but is dependent on the nature of relation between them?"

I said, "Yes, we can say that the love brings two things together, reducing their (perception of) separation, whereas the hate or dislike moves the two things apart, increasing their (perception of) separation."

There was more to it. It is not simply a matter of our likes, dislikes, pleasures or pain. There was something more fundamental. It had something to do with our desires and intentions. As long as one has some desire to do something, one will have to make some efforts to fulfil those desires. The process of making effort needs energy. When one makes efforts, one gets tired in the process. The amount of effort applied in achieving the desired end-goals also seems to affect the perception of separation.

I said, "Not all situations can be described in terms of likes, dislikes, pleasures or pain. But at all times you are sure about how much effort you are putting in a task or a relation. The perception of the separation depends on the amount of effort you apply in achieving some end goal. When you were asked to check on the pressure cooker, you had to put some efforts. This made the wait seem to last so long. Had it been an act of

184

watching a television program of your choice, you would have put no effort. The time would have swiftly passed."

Maya asked, "Is there a limit on how much this separation can be felt between the two things or people?"

I asked her, "You mean to say how long a time gap you can experience or how close you could come to something?"

Maya said, "Sort of."

I asked, "What would you say if I say that there is no limit to this perception of separation. It extended from zero to infinity."

Maya said with disbelief, "What? How can you experience something like a zero or infinity?"

I said, "Yes, you do. We do experience both of them, many times in our days. It's a different thing we are not aware of that."

Maya was not even sure about this. She waited for me to say more.

I asked her, "What is eternity?"

Maya said, "Eternity is like infinity, perpetuity, or endlessness."

I said, "Or timelessness."

Maya said, "Sure."

I asked her, "And when do we say we experience it?"

Maya said, "When something is taking forever, we say it feels like eternity."

I said, "True. When you are made to do some effort that you don't like much, you feel extremely bored and feel as if it is going to take forever. Like a never-ending task."

Maya said, "Yes. Something like this."

I asked, "Can you imagine something never ending, lasting forever, infinite?"

Maya said, "Not actually. It is because it will always be greater than the biggest I can imagine or measure."

I asked her, "Has it ever occurred to you that something could be never-ending or endless not because it was immensely big but because one could not see or measure its end?"

Maya said, "No. When we talk about something being endless, we imagine it going on and on forever without its ends being noticeable."

I said, "This is why I have brought a very different perspective to our usual understanding of eternity or infinity. When you look at anything in this way, you will find that eternity or infinity has nothing to do with the immense magnitude of separation in space or time. All you need for something to be infinite or eternal is the inability to measure it. In such case, when you cannot measure the separation, you have no idea about the magnitude."

Maya said, "Hmm. I never thought about it."

I said, "Something infinite or eternal is something immeasurable. It could be either too large to be measured or it was never measured. In both the cases, the thing will be seen or felt as infinite and the time duration will be felt like eternity."

Maya asked, "What are you trying to say?"

I said, "I am saying that an unmeasured space or interval is same as unmeasurable space or interval. The idea of separation between two things or events is seen in terms of big and small, or far and near. It can be easily seen that in love the distance seems to disappear and in hate the distance seems to grow. We tend to feel the distance in space or time growing huge if we do not like something. This is evident in terms of ignoring the presence or interaction with people or things we do not like. When you were asked to look after the pressure cooker which was not an interesting task for you, you found the time of wait to be long. You could as well feel this time of wait as an eternity, because you had no idea about how long the process was going to take. On the other side, if you had been asked to spend fifteen minutes to watch your favorite show on the television, you would have found this time to passed very quickly."

Maya said, "In love, likes and pleasures the distance in space and time shrinks. In hate, dislikes and pain, the distance in space and time expands. Is that right?"

I said, "Yes, that is right."

Maya smiled.

I said, "This is only a part of the problem. We have only talked about our perception of the time as a separation

187

between the two events. Before we even talk about the time gap between two events, we should find out if we even understand the meaning of the time at any moment."

Maya said, "Is it not the time right now that is called the present moment?"

I said, "Yes, it is. But we seem to divide the time into three zones, such as past, present and the future."

Maya said, "Is that not right? What has already happened is called the past. What has not yet happened is called the future."

I asked her, "Is there any time when you are not in the present moment? Can you imagine at any moment when you are not 'here' but somewhere else?"

Maya said, "That would be ridiculous to say that I can be anywhere but here and now at any moment."

I said, "If you cannot be anywhere or at any other place but where you are at that moment, what is the nature of the thing called as past or future? Is that a reality or an illusion?"

Maya didn't say anything. She didn't know what to say. The answer was obvious, but it was not how everyone experienced. We all have been living in our lives based on time intervals, days and calendars scheduling and planning our activities. We are hardly ever experiencing the reality in the present moment. We are always busy in our thoughts, which are either of the past, or of the future.

Maya said, "It might be right, but how could someone be only in the present moment and not be aware of the past memory or the future expectations? Won't it be like a death for an ordinary person?"

I asked, "What did we say about someone in love?"

Maya said, "You had said that in love there is no separation in time and space. We talked about a mother feeling close to her child irrespective of physical distance between the two. We also talked about our lost sense of time when doing something we love very much."

I said, "True. In love there is no separation. What does it mean to have no separation? We said that if there is no separation between two things, then there are actually no two things. There will be only one thing in absence of separation. The mother and her son are not really two. They are simply one. It is true under all circumstances. In (pure) love, there is only one thing, not two or more. In the same way, there is no separation in time too when there is love. What does it mean to have no separation in time? There is no separation in the sense that there is no idea of past, present or future as separation. There is only one time, the present moment, when there is love."

Maya said, "I don't understand how there is no past, present or future when there is love."

I said, "It cannot be explained. Neither it can be understood by mere listening. There is no logical or intellectual reasoning to make one understand the meaning of eternity, infinity or simply love by mere words. The only way is to be in love, and to experience the dissolving of all time. When this happens, all separation in space and time is lost. What one experiences on losing one's individuality and the sense of time

189

in pure love cannot be understood by others. That which might be an experience of pure ecstasy by someone in love would be seen as nothing but as a death by ordinary people."

Maya said, "I can agree. It would not be simple for someone to understand the love that the mother has for her child. Love cannot be understood. It can only be experienced."

I said, "So, we said that all separation between various objects and events is simply an illusion depending on our efforts and experiences. All pleasurable and effortless experiences seem to shrink the time while all the effortful and hurting experiences seem to expand the time. The separation between two individuals is also not dependent on their physical separation. It depends on the depth of their relationship."

Maya said, "And we are saying that the separation in space and time is an illusion because a physical separation does not correspond to the separation perceived in reality."

I said, "All separation is an illusion. Not only is it an illusion because it does not correspond to the physical separation, but it is also an illusion because the separation in space and time are dynamic in nature. They can change based on our perception of pain, pleasure and efforts."

Maya asked, "When you say that the separation can change, do you mean to say that what was far away can come close too?"

I said, "Yes. All separation is an illusion. It is dependent on our perception of pain and pleasure. It is possible for the separation to go from infinity to zero in an instant."

Maya said, "I don't believe it! How can something change from infinity to zero in an instant?"

I said, "It does. When you have an enmity with someone, the separation between you two is infinite. It is possible that the cause of the enmity is some misunderstanding. At some point of time, it is possible for the misunderstanding to go away, leading to dissolution of all separation between the two instantly."

Maya said, "Oh! I see. This way even the opposite must be true. I can say this because I and Christina were very good friends for so many years. It was only one misunderstanding that made us get separated in an instant."

I said, "You will agree that the idea of separation between objects and people is nothing but an illusion. This separation not only has its roots in our individual perception of efforts, pains and pleasures, but is also very dynamic in nature."

Maya said, "I can understand it now. All our ideas of friendship or enmity are simply illusions. Our ideas of separation from one another, of superiority from other people or species is also an illusion. If we were in true love with the existence, then there was no separation between us and the other species. In such a state, there was no idea of time in terms of past experiences or future expectations. In such a state, the whole illusion of time and space is also non-existent."

I said, "Until that happens, the illusion of time and space is very much a reality."

Summarizing Illusions

Objects, separation, knowledge, birth, death, duality, time and space, none of it is how it is perceived.

I asked Maya if she had understood the meaning of her name. She smiled. She said that more than the meaning of her name, she was able to realize the delusions we humans had about the universe we live in.

I asked her if she could write a short summary about how our world was an illusion. She was happy that I asked her. She spent a few hours in her room working with the different notes she had prepared all this time we talked about it. The next day she came and showed me what all she had collected from our discussion about the nature of our universe. She wrote,

"An illusion means perceiving the world different than what it is. At no time can we really know that our perceptions might not be the reality. It is only later that one can know about the experiences that felt real at some time were illusions It won't be wrong to say that all illusions were once a reality.

The reality is a never-ending chaotic movement of different elements in the nature. There is no division anywhere in the reality, either in time or space. Yet, the human mind, unable to understand the random nature of reality creates imaginary divisions and regularity so that it can predict and control the nature more easily.

If we see a continuously changing pattern, then imagining a fixed shape among the random motion is an illusion. Looking at the clouds and seeing a lion or a face of a girl is such an imagination. They are illusion because they are temporary by nature. We are aware that everything in the nature is under a transformation. A seedling emerges from the earth and continues to appear as a growing shape in front of our eyes. That which we see as a plant, growing on to become a tree full of tough branches, soft leaves, colorful flowers and sweet fruits is nothing but a transformation originating from the earth. The same structure which we call as a tree eventually dries out and becomes part of the earth again. If we fast forward the whole sequence from the time the seedling started growing to the time the tree has vanished in the earth, we can separate the illusion from the facts. The fact was that all such transformations happened in time. The illusion was the naming and recognizing of those changes as the things known as seeds, leaves, branches, flowers, death and birth.

The changes such as the earth's transformation of becoming the leaves, flowers, fruits and the branches are seen everywhere else too in the nature. The same happens with bees, butterflies, fish, bacteria, dogs and humans alike. The content of the bodies of all animals, plants and rocks are not different from the planet we live on. Neither are they different from a distant planet millions of light years far from the earth. What is a finger on our body at this moment, might be found in parts of a tree's leaves, a dog's nose, a fish's eyes and a rock on a mountain in a few thousand years from now. We can see and feel such illusion in the miniature cities of plastic blocks we make in an amusement park where the pieces continue to change place to become part of a toy building, or a miniature boat, or a little person's hat over a period of time.

The illusion of naming and recognizing objects, things and people in the ever-transforming reality is not the major concern. They are like identifying faces on the rocks or naming and identifying random objects as having a personality. The real problem is the nature of our mind to get attached to those things once they have been identified (with name and form). The attachment to those things which feel real due to the illusion makes is difficult for us to see them get transformed and destroyed later. The reality is that there was no such thing in the beginning before they were born to be identified and get attached with. The illusion of a thing as a real 'thing' makes it harder for us to let go when they die. In reality, there was neither the birth or a death. But in ignorance, we experience the illusory realities of birth as well as the sufferings of the death in such transformations. It is similar to the real experiences of joy or sorrow watching a movie forgetting that everything is just a play of the artists.

Human mind is unable to understand anything in absolute terms. It can only perceive and understand different things in comparison to fixed references. The different standard symbols and their values imagined and created for such purposes allow us to quantify all the things in relative terms. We can know how long or short something is in relation to other, or how heavy or light it is. The feeling of pain, heat, hunger, temperature, density, and about any other sensation we can know, are all in relative terms. Unable to really grasp absolute nature of anything, we are satisfied with just the relative understanding of reality, which at best, creates a distorted view of our universe.

Though we might never know our perceptions to be of illusory at the time of experiencing reality, we can probably see it clearly later. Looking at the pattern of previous illusory experiences, one can establish some ground rules that set reality apart from illusions.

Illusions exist in the following cases:
1) Perceiving a form when there is none
2) Perceiving a movement when there is none
3) Perceiving a meaning when there is none
4) Creating a reality by perceiving a thing for another
5) Creating a reality from an idea, without even perceiving

The world that we live in is full of actions. Everything is moving, merging and segregating at all the times. Every action leads to another in the never-ending game of life. It is not easy to ascertain if there is any real actor behind the actions we notice at every moment or if the idea of an actor is a mere illusion. It would seem easy to find the root of all movement by looking at all such actions which depend on other causes. Anything which can be identified as the main cause of further action, cannot ever depend on any other cause. All other intermediate actions must simply be the mode to transfer the initial action through different mediums acting as dependencies. Yet, when one tries to trace back the sequence of dependent actions in this world, one cannot find a single cause solely responsible for any action in this universe. There is not a single entity that acts without a purpose. If at all there was something which could be identified as an independent cause of any action, it would be an unconditioned intent, a purposeless act. A conditioned intent, on the contrary, cannot be a root cause of actions because it depends on its conditioning to cause further actions.

Illusion of a perceived actor behind any action is easily broken when one identifies and rejects all actions which are dependent on other causes. If the cause of a murder is a wound made by a knife, and the attack using the knife is caused by a person, it needs to be found further if the person had any motive behind the murder. The motive of the killing might be poverty and hunger. It is easy to hold the person accountable for the murder and punish him, but it does not stop more murders from happening. With every new murder, we will continue to punish another person forever if we do not try to go further in our search for the real actor behind such actions. Instead, if the root cause behind the crimes is explored and found to be the hunger and the problem of hunger was solved, a considerable reduction in the numbers of future murders could be seen. Our laws have been there for a long time for violence, rapes, murders and driving under influence, yet we don't see if our laws and their enforcement have made any significant impact on reducing the number of similar crimes in future.

We continue to interact in this world with different species and objects, treating them as being individual and singular. We assume that they are not only single and separate entities, but they also have an independent existence. Yet on a closer inspection, we fail to find a single independent entity in the whole universe. We consider our bodies as single structure, yet we know that it is made up of billions of smaller parts.

Likewise, every other known thing in this universe is made up of countless smaller units. In fact, all objects are really assemblies; they are made up of other smaller parts, which are further assemblies of even smaller parts. The illusion that an object is a single entity results from our assumption and an expectation that it has a permanent existence. We expect things to continue retaining their constituents and their characteristics for a long time. Yet, when the parts which make it up as a single structure, separate into smaller assemblies and divisions, we see this transition or transformation as a destruction of the original object. Entangled in the illusion of objects as single entity and our never-ending attachment for them, we continue to suffer their disintegration due to diseases, accidents or aging.

There are no objects that are isolated from each other. There is, instead, a continuous interaction and exchange of particles between various things in this universe. Besides the idea of individual objects among myriad of assemblies continuously exchanging their member particles, we are also confused that the objects are separable from the properties they exhibit. We fail to understand that the objects are not simply the containers which can add, possess or get rid of some or all their qualities. There are no separate identifiable objects in this universe apart from their properties. It is, in fact, a group of properties that we perceive and assign names and shape to recognize them as objects. Once we have solidified the idea of objects, we imagine them to exhibit all such properties which we perceived in our initial interaction.

When we form an illusory idea of objects containing some properties or people exhibiting some behavioral traits, we start assuming that it must be easy for things to drop some of their behavior. An object or a thing is not different than the

198

properties it exhibits. A person is not detached from his thoughts. It is not easy to convince a religious person to change his faith. To change one's habit is like a death to a person. If you take the heat away from the sun, the sun experiences death. If you take the God away from a religious person, you kill the person (from inside). It is only under severe crisis that a human decides to change or transform. Otherwise, under ordinary circumstances, it is a wishful thinking to make oneself come out of one's comfort zone or to apply out-of-box thinking to critically solve a problem.

One of the biggest illusion we have is the imaginary separation between different things in this universe. We continue to live our lives among different people, species and objects assuming everything as separate and independent of everything else. We hardly ever realize that not a single atom in this universe has an independent and separate existence. We all are made of everything that our planet is made of. We breathe the same air that goes through the bodies of everyone else. We share the resources, habits and emotions with the rest of the lives on the planet. We continue to exchange our contents, our ideas and our weaknesses with all other species and objects of the universe. Until we realize our inter-dependence with each other serving a bigger universal role, we will continue to live a broken existence, a life of suffering.

We continue to learn and get educated believing that intelligence is in direct relation to the knowledge we gather from books, teachers and previous experiences of the human-kind. Our illusory ideas about knowledge and intelligence makes us behave in the most bizarre ways where we think that intelligence can be individually broken down, measured or cultivated through our limited actions in this world. We cannot come to the simple conclusion that no knowledge is ever complete. There have been numerous examples where past knowledge and theories have been proven wrong at a later time by scientists and scholars.

When we live in a community and interact with different people through our langue and behavior, we tend to create our own internal biases which makes us see the world divided into two parts, one which we consider as ours and the other which we do not consider ours. In creating such artificial and imaginary division, we tend to look at everything with a divided view, giving a higher weightage to the things and acts belonging to us as opposed to the rest. While we view the different things, we look at those more favorably which we consider ours, whereas we feel a little alienated towards those which we don't consider our own. With such distorted vision we create a skewed and broken image of the world we live in. We see it broken, we communicate it broken and we experience it as a broken reality. Living this way, we fail to see that such an interpretation of the world is an imagination of our minds.

We look at different things being born or facing death at every moment. We do not realize that the nature of birth and death is nothing but an illusion of the mind. In reality, that which takes birth is simply an idea made up from the creation of a name and form in the awareness of the mind. If paid complete attention, a person becomes completely free of the realm of births and deaths. It is the inattention that makes a person fall in the trap of identification, association and attachment in this worldly drama.

Our minds are dualistic; they tend to get cornered in the extreme ends of all opposites. In terms of emotions we either understand happiness or sorrow. If we are happy with something and suddenly get hurt, we change position to the other end to experience hurt, enmity and anger. We don't know the middle ground of simply being not happy without falling in the trap of being hateful. We invent two sides of everything in our quest of understanding reality, whereas the fact is that the very act of trying to understand something through opposites turns it into an illusion. The mind's dualistic nature makes it impossible to understand anything that does not have opposites. In other words, everything the mind understands, must be of dualistic nature. In an ideal world free of illusion, a free person wouldn't know what freedom is, so would a humble person not know of humility."

I said, "Wow! This is really good."

Maya looked at me. She was not sure. She said, "I don't feel comfortable. It looks like a hyperbole. It looks like I am trying to speak big words. It doesn't look like I will be able to make others understand all this, even though I am myself convinced with every single word I am saying.

I said, "There is another way to express difficult ideas and emotions. You could try writing a poem."

She came to me next day with a poem.

[On Separation]
The bees are animated, they fly, buzz and sting
The flowers are still, grounded to the earth.
Each one is separate, individual and alone
Yet they are really One in this wonderous world.

201

If the bees and flowers were separate,
then why should flowers die when bees are no more?

[On Knowledge]
I am intelligent, you are stupid
I can solve math problem and you can't read a word
I can buy a house, a boat and lots of clothes
And you can hardly manage a roof over your hut
I suffer stress, can't find time and struggle to sleep
While you laugh, enjoy and sleep on the bed of rocks

[On Personal Bias]
You tell me something and I don't get it
I show you this and you don't see that
You ask me a question and I suffer intimidation
I offer you food and you can't satisfy your hunger
You and I are so far away, the ridge is so deep
It can only be filled, by dead body of yours or mine

[On Objects and Personality]
The sun cannot lose heat and still be a sun
The flower cannot lose colors and still be flower
The food cannot lose taste and still be food
Yet, you lose temper and think you are still you.

                                        -Maya, the Grand Illusion

Printed in Great Britain
by Amazon

29917381R00117